BREAK BREAD ON A BUDGET

BREAK BREAD ON A BUDGET

Ordinary Ingredients, Extraordinary Meals

Lexy Rogers

Row House Publishing recognizes that the power of justice-centered storytelling isn't a phenomenon; it is essential for progress. We believe in equity and activism, and that books—and the culture around them—have the potential to transform the universal conversation around what it means to be human.

Thank you for being an important part of the conversation and holding sacred the critical work of our authors.

DESIGNED BY PAULINE NEUWIRTH, NEUWIRTH & ASSOCIATES, INC.

Library of Congress Cataloging-in-Publication Data Available Upon Request
ISBN 978-1-955-90523-7 (TP)
ISBN 978-1-955-90524-4 (eBook)
Printed in the United States
Distributed by Simon & Schuster
First edition
10 9 8 7 6 5 4 3 2 1

I couldn't have done this alone, so here's to my biggest influences:

I dedicate this book to Mama Anne and Auntie Lovie. You both showed me that food is more than just nutrition, it's bite-sized pieces of love.

And to my husband, Lewis, for believing in me when I have trouble believing in myself.

CONTENTS

FOOD IS MY LOVE LANGUAGE.

Years before I was a contestant on *Master-Chef*, before I became a wife to Lewis Rogers and a mother to Luke, Lena, and Luna Rogers, I fell in love with cooking. At eight years old, I remember being on my tippy toes, peering over the counter to get a peek at my Auntie Lovie and grandma (we all call her Mama Anne) making magic in our tiny, rustic kitchen. It was an effortless alchemy. In a buzz of noisy, joyful chaos, Auntie Lovie and Mama Anne expressed their love for our family by turning everyday ingredients into extraordinary, heavenly smelling, warm-your-belly, hearty, nourishing meals.

Sure, Mama Anne and Auntie Lovie showed me how to make the perfect collard greens and fried corn. But they also instilled in me a deeper lesson about connection and community.

In our home, food had the power to bring people together, soothe weary souls, brighten someone's day, and shape the dreams of a curious eight-year-old child. Mama Anne and her husband, Papa Fred, had a way of making strangers feel like family. Aromas from our kitchen wafted through the neighborhood, bringing people from all down the block right to our doorstep for a phenomenal plate of food. Thanks to the aroma-filled, warm-bellied childhood memories created by Mama Anne and Auntie Lovie, cooking for others became my love language, one that I now express to my husband, my children, and my community.

Later, during my late-night college cooking sessions in the dorm kitchen, I discovered my talent for throwing together creative dishes with whatever we had on hand. My college experience brought me two very important things: my hubby, Lewis (aka the love of my life and true best friend), and the confidence that I can throw down in the kitchen.

Lewis and I were determined to spend every lovely, hectic, uncertain, and undiscovered day together for the rest of our lives. When we got married, we said "I do" to building a foundation of generational wealth for our kids and their kids. So, we made a pact and a strict budget. My taste buds are bougie, but my pockets are stingy.

From this bougie/stingy/generational alchemist place, the highly controversial $40-per-week grocery budget (the one Gordon Ramsay and everyone else on *MasterChef* couldn't stop talking about) was born. To answer your question, yes. Yes, I did actually spend only $40 per week on groceries. To be fair, it was mainly my husband and me doing the eating. But any pregnant/nursing mother can confirm that those babies consumed a healthy share of calories through their mama. Does that make my grocery budgeting abilities any less impressive? I'll let you decide.

When my season of *MasterChef* aired, some said I was labeling myself as a "poor Black girl" and acting like my personal budget was a public weakness. I am ashamed to say it affected me more than it should have. But I am not ashamed anymore, and if you can relate to my story, you shouldn't be ashamed either. We live in a time of food deserts (lack of affordable, nutritious foods in marginalized communities). Systemic oppression forces people to rely on SNAP benefits to feed their children, even though they work full-time jobs. Wages have stalled while living expenses have skyrocketed. I say "HECK NO" to that nonsense. I'm proud of my ingenuity in the kitchen.

I'm not a "poor Black girl." I am the architect of my children's phenomenal future. Besides, budget food can taste amazing if you know how to use the ingredients right. I don't need saffron and wagyu steak. I have Auntie Lovie and Mama Anne's legacy.

Over time, I've developed my own version of weekly meal prep, lining up ingredients to use in multiple dishes in the same week to ensure nothing goes to waste. My grocery lists are meticulous and strategically designed. Now, I'm passing this knowledge to you. *Break Bread on a Budget* will not only give you extraordinary recipes from ordinary ingredients, but it will also teach you how to plan and prep your meals without a single crumb of wasted food.

This book is my passion—no, my LOVE project. *Break Bread on a Budget* is my sincere offering and enthusiastic answer to people who, after seeing me on *MasterChef*, asked me for my recipes and tips on how to cook on a budget. My fancy chef friends may not appreciate some of these recipes, and that's okay. Canned foods are cheaper. Premade biscuit dough is easier. This book is for parents with toddlers clinging to their legs, folks saving pennies for their kids' tuition, and college students craving easy, inexpensive late-night food. I see you.

Aside from offering carefully crafted, yummy, easy-to-make, affordable recipes, I hooked y'all up! In this book, you'll also find grocery lists, charts, tables, tips, and tricks; so you can cook food *easily and affordably*.

When I picture families and communities all over the country breaking bread together, like we used to do in Mama Anne's kitchen, it fills me with incredible joy. Whether you cook to live or live to cook, these simple yet delicious meals are easy to make, fun to enjoy, and full of heart.

With love and power,
Lexy Rogers

TIPS AND TRICKS

COOKING IS PERSONAL. WHAT I love most about cooking is how unique it is for each person. Every home cook or chef has a particular way of doing things. Culture, location, and personality all profoundly impact the way we create and what we prioritize in the kitchen. These tips and tricks are my treasured tidbits of kitchen wisdom, cultivated since my childhood in Mama Anne's kitchen and expanded upon as I've learned new skills in adulthood.

Now, some of you might think of cooking as a messy, time-consuming, tedious chore. I get it. You spend all that time chopping, frying, roasting, and creating a meal that your picky toddler may or may not eat, and the rest of your family devours it in five minutes. It may seem like a ton of work for little reward. While I won't argue that dishwashing is an abomination, I will say that cooking can be more fulfilling than you think. That brings us to my first tip.

1. Enjoy the process. Put on some music and have an adventure with your ingredients. Without a shadow of a doubt, I truly believe that love can transform a dish. Joy can be tasted, felt, and even seen in our food. When food doesn't live up to the hype at a restaurant, my first thought is that the chef is probably having a bad day. When you step into your kitchen and fire up your stove, take a moment to appreciate the ingredients in front of you. Applaud yourself for your courage and dedication. Those fast-food joints don't care about your experience, and they're not putting you first. Somebody needs to make you the priority that you are.

    Cook because you deserve it. Cook because only you can make something unique and specifically crafted to your tastes and preferences. A healthy and happy relationship with your ingredients makes all the difference in your final dish.

2. Ditch the daily grocery list. A healthy relationship with your ingredients starts with streamlining your grocery shopping process. There are many ways to organize a shopping list. Some people shop for the whole month, stocking up on bulk items that ultimately get tossed or lost in the freezer. Some shop a little every day, grabbing ingredients on their way home from work as part of their daily routine.

    I used to organize my lists in a "logical" way. I looked through the cabinets, checked the freezer and refrigerator, and made a list of items we needed based on what was gone or almost gone. The only problem is that I *always* found myself going back to the store for a few things to make that night's meal. Those quick grocery runs right before dinnertime are mentally and physically draining, especially with kids in tow. When we're tired, we're more inclined to order out, which can put a huge strain on the wallet. Cooking is supposed to be joyful, not stressful and tiring.

Words to the wise:

- *Never* go grocery shopping on an empty stomach. It's almost impossible to avoid buying items you don't need when shopping while hungry. If you must do a last-minute grocery stop, snack on a granola bar so your stomach's not the one doing the buying.
- Don't attempt a big, complicated cooking session while tired. I have some low-stress,

quick meals to get you through those days. (See page 175 for my 30-minute meals.)

THE MENU-FIRST APPROACH

Monthly and biweekly meal planning is too much commitment for me. Instead, I create my menu for the week *before* I organize my shopping list. A weekly menu is perfect for my family, but feel free to adjust your timeframe to whatever works best for you.

Here's a rundown of my process:

- *Plan a weekly menu.* I choose one day (usually Saturday) to sit down, look through saved recipes, and listen to my body to decide what I want to eat. Then I plan my menu for the week. This method gives me peace of mind and addresses the dreaded question: "So, what's for dinner tonight?"
- *Make a grocery list based on my menu.* I create an ingredient list based on the recipes for my menu. Organizing the list this way allows you to tailor your meals according to your budget for that week. Life happens. Some weeks may have more wiggle room in the budget than others. I can just as easily feed my family of five on $40 a week as I can on $200 a week when I plan meals this way.
- *List the staple items.* Aside from the menu ingredients, there are some items you should *always* have in your kitchen. If you stock your kitchen properly, you should be able to make three to five meals with random items in your pantry at any given moment. I'm not a "doomsday prepper," but I do see the value in being able to feed your family in a pinch. There have been plenty of nights when we've either been between paychecks or recovering from a financial emergency and needed

to nourish the family without spending extra money.

STAPLE ITEMS AND HOW TO USE THEM

Ramen: This glorious college staple is a favorite in my household. We love to make our ramen with a soft-boiled egg, chopped green onions, crispy fried onion straws, and shrimp. The add-ins are numerous, making this a quick, affordable meal that can please the whole family in minutes.

Uncooked noodles: Like ramen, pasta is undeniably one of the most versatile ingredients out there. Whether you are a pesto, tomato, or cream-based sauce person, you can't have a pasta dish without noodles. (Don't worry, we'll get into pasta making later.)

Heavy cream: In my house, heavy cream is a necessity. If you want to make most of the sauces in this book, you need heavy cream. This stuff is the best. It has an expiration date that far surpasses regular milk, and it's incredibly versatile. You can use it to replace anything from butter to whipped cream to Alfredo sauce. For us, heavy cream is as much a pantry staple as flour, sugar, and eggs.

Butter: Butter equals flavor. It can be used for roux (we'll dive into those later), folded into eggs (check out the perfect scrambled egg recipe), and added to sauces for a rich velvet finish. I grab a pack of butter every other trip to the store if our budget allows. I use what I need and freeze the rest. I will never allow us to run out of butter.

Frozen meats: When I have a little extra money to spend, I invest in meats that can be stored in my freezer for months at a time. Ground beef, steaks, and roasts will last for about four months in the freezer.

Most fish and shrimp last three to six months in the freezer. Then there's chicken for the win, lasting nine months to a whole year in your freezer. Stock up on meats when you can, so you always have something in your freezer for the months ahead.*

Rice: Man, oh man, this is a big one! A five-pound bag of rice that costs five bucks can last half a year, and it goes with everything! My family's favorite is vegetable fried rice. Pop open a bag of medley veggies, crack open a few eggs, add soy sauce and seasonings, and—bam—dinner is served. To be even more basic, rice and chicken is a whole meal, people. Season it properly, plate it pretty, and even the best chefs wouldn't be mad at your budget-friendly dinner choice.

Tony Chachere's Creole Seasoning (readily available in most major food chains and big-box stores): Let me preface by saying this company does not sponsor me. I just love their seasoning. It's a staple for any home chef, whether you have a perfect sense of smell, depth of palate, and understanding of food compositions or not. This seasoning will save all meals from being bland, boring, and uninspired.

Potatoes: Potatoes are a great filler ingredient. Add roasted, mashed, fondant, or baked potatoes to any meal to fill the belly on a budget.

Onions: Onions are a versatile ingredient that can transform almost any dish from boring to bold.

Fresh basil and rosemary plants: What good are budget meals if they're bland? Save costs on key herbs by buying a plant instead of packaged herbs. We keep our herb plants on the windowsill in our kitchen. Take care of them and they will take care of you. Our basil plant is still flourishing, years after I bought it.

Green onions/scallions: This slightly sweeter onion is an ingredient I add in most dishes. Use it as a garnish to feel extra accomplished in your final product or add it into scrambled eggs with a touch of crème fraîche. However you choose to utilize these green stalks of flavor, you will not be disappointed.

> **Pro tip:** Did you know you can put your green onions in a mason jar of water, and they will grow back? We've been doing this for years now. Best 70 cents we ever invested.

Tailor your pantry staples to your individual taste. The staples I've listed are personal to me and are included in the majority of the recipes in this book. However, feel free to substitute any of my staples for ones that you and your family will enjoy and that suit your lifestyle best. The main idea is to always have your core ingredients on hand so you'll be more motivated to cook from home.

* **Note:** If you are vegetarian or vegan, frozen veggies are also a must. Most vegetables are freezer-friendly for up to one year.

CUSTOM-MADE GROCERY LISTS AND WEEKLY MENUS

HERE YOU'LL FIND GROCERY LISTS that correspond to weekly menus I put together, which correspond to the recipes in this book. Girl, didn't I tell you I got you?! Each list is organized to properly utilize the ingredients needed for a week's worth of meals. Let me help you jump-start your at-home cooking adventure. Simply pick a list, grab your groceries, and let this book do the rest.

Note that these menus are for a work week (Monday–Friday). This was intentional. Weekends are when we spend the most intentional time together, whether that's visiting friends and family, going for hikes, or spending the day at an amusement park. That also means they are usually the days we eat out the most. I noticed this trend with others as well and decided it best to leave the weekend up to you. This gives you flexibility and keeps you from spending money on groceries you might not use.

❤ MENU #1 ❤

These recipes are for the ones who cook from home for every meal of the day and need a little break from decision fatigue. I present:

THE SAHP (STAY-AT-HOME PARENT)

	MONDAY	TUESDAY	WEDNESDAY	THURSDAY	FRIDAY
BREAKFAST	Mini Frittatas (page 49)	Leftovers (relax and unwind)	Happier-Than-Ever Hash (page 50)	Soft-Boiled Egg and Avocado Toast (page 53)	Luke's Monkey Bread (page 70)
LUNCH	(Julius) Caesar Dressing/Salad (pages 105–6)	Leftovers	Joey's Meatball Sub (page 90)	Anything-but-Basic Tomato Soup (page 78)	Lemon Garlic–Infused Olive Oil/Salad (pages 110–13)
DINNER	The Louise Dip Soup (page 82)	Leftovers	Lasagna Roll-Ups (page 173)	Leftovers of your choice	Not-from-Philly Cheesesteak (page 89)

Feel free to swap the leftover day to whichever day suits your needs that week.

THE SAHP MENU GROCERY LIST

5 white onions

4 red onions

5 green bell peppers

4 red bell peppers

1 yellow bell peppers

1 orange bell peppers

8 ounces baby bella mushrooms

1 head romaine lettuce

I head iceberg lettuce

1 sweet potato

1 lemon

Olives

Capers

Avocado (the recipe calls for 1, but the more you buy, the more you can make)

40 ounces cherry or grape tomatoes

10 ounces fresh spinach

Bread for toast

1 loaf French bread

10 hoagie rolls

Bread crumbs (Italian-flavored)

Croutons

4 pounds Italian pork sausage

8 ounces ground beef

1 pound shaved steak

4 ounces canned anchovies

24 ounces marinara sauce

28 ounces whole tomatoes

1 tablespoon sun-dried tomatoes

2 cups chicken broth

10 ounces RO-TEL diced tomatoes and green chiles

1 box lasagna noodles

2 cans biscuits

2 dozen eggs

8 ounces shredded cheddar cheese

24 ounces Italian blend shredded cheese

Two 16-ounce packs provolone cheese slices

12 slices pepper Jack cheese

3 packages cream cheese (12 ounces total)

16 ounces ricotta cheese

Grated Parmesan cheese

Heavy cream

STAPLES, SEASONINGS, AND HERBS

Butter

Salt

Pepper

Italian seasonings

Rosemary

Olive oil and avocado oil (avocado oil optional)

Garlic powder

Onion powder

Red pepper flakes

White sugar

Brown sugar

Ground cinnamon

Vanilla extract

Dried parsley

Heads of garlic (or jarred minced garlic)

Creole seasoning (I prefer Tony Chachere's)

Chives

Basil

Worcestershire sauce

Dijon mustard

Chicken bouillon cubes

Lemon pepper seasoning

Paprika

♥ MENU #2 ♥

This list proves that it truly pays to be a penny-pincher. Introducing:

THE BUDGET BUILDER

	MONDAY	TUESDAY	WEDNESDAY	THURSDAY	FRIDAY
DINNER	Not Ya Mama's Chili (page 81)	Fettuccine Alfredo (page 170)	Cream Cheese-Stuffed Baked Chicken and Veggie Medley (page 136)	Cheddar Broccoli Soup (page 77)	Leftovers

THE BUDGET BUILDER MENU GROCERY LIST

2 red onions

2 white onions

1 yellow onion

1 green pepper

1 yellow pepper

1 red pepper

1 zucchini

1 yellow squash

10-ounce bag matchstick carrots

16 ounces frozen broccoli

30 ounces black beans

30 ounces dark red kidney beans

30 ounces pinto beans

14.5 ounces fire-roasted tomatoes

30 ounces tomato sauce

1.5 pounds pork sausage or ground beef (optional)

2.5 pounds chicken breast

32 ounces heavy cream

2 packages cream cheese (12 ounces total)

16 ounces shredded Colby Jack cheese

16 ounces shredded cheddar cheese

1 box fettuccine noodles (check out page 160 for a fresh noodle recipe)

3 cups chicken broth

STAPLES, SEASONINGS, AND HERBS

Garlic powder

Onion powder

Butter

Freeze-dried chives

Pepper

Salt

Lemon pepper seasoning

Olive oil

Minced garlic

Dried oregano

Ground cayenne pepper

♥ MENU #3 ♥

This list is for the weeks full of meetings, homework, or terrible twos! Introducing:

EASY-PEASY LEMON SQUEEZY

	MONDAY	TUESDAY	WEDNESDAY	THURSDAY	FRIDAY
DINNER	Hot Honey Sautéed Chicken (page 139)	One-Pot Chicken Thighs (page 185)	Cabbage Steaks (page 181)	Smothered Pork Chops and Rice (page 178)	Quick One-Sheet Salmon (page 144)

THE EASY-PEASY LEMON SQUEEZY MENU GROCERY LIST

1 white onion

1 yellow onion

1 red onion

1 red pepper

1 yellow pepper

1 green pepper

3 russet potatoes

1 large head cabbage

Baby bella mushrooms

2 pounds asparagus

1 lemon

2 pounds salmon

2 pounds chicken tenders

1.5-2 pounds chicken thighs, bone out

2 pounds thin sliced pork chops

0.5 ounce salami

2 cups rice

1 cup chicken broth

8 ounces canned marinara

Heavy cream

Sesame seeds (optional garnish)

Grated Parmesan cheese

4 ounces mozzarella

STAPLES, SEASONINGS, AND HERBS

Rosemary (fresh plant)

Basil (fresh plant)

Old Bay seasoning

Freeze-dried chives

Cayenne pepper

Paprika

Corn starch

Butter

Salt

Pepper

Lemon pepper seasoning

Grapeseed oil (canola oil will work as a substitute)

UNFORTUNATELY, KITCHENS DON'T COME with a manual. Honestly, we should talk to someone about that. Maybe your culinary knowledge ends with how to use a microwave. No shame in that! Or maybe you're already a pro, looking for a quick refresher on kitchen fundamentals. There is something for everyone in this section. Use it for reference as you master the recipes in this book and show off your new skills to your friends.

BASIC KNIFE SKILLS

Any chef will tell you that the key to efficiency in the kitchen is the mastery of knife skills. We're growing, glowing, thriving, and jiving individuals. We cannot afford to spend 20 minutes chopping onions, honey!

Here's a list of your basic, need-to-know knife skills:

DICE

As the name implies, dicing is the process of cutting food into, well, the shape of dice. The sizes vary from large, medium, small, or brunoise (tiny). To dice, cut your ingredient both horizontally and vertically to create a cube, usually about ¼-inch in size.

ROUGH CHOP

I like to think of the rough chop as rustic cutting. You'll get a less-precise cut and a slightly-larger-than-average dice with rough chopping.

Dice

Rough Chop

JULIENNE

Julienne is the process of cutting an ingredient into thin, matchstick-like pieces.

CHIFFONADE

I use the chiffonade technique almost every day with basil leaves. (Fun fact: your girl has a serious love affair with fresh basil.) This cutting method requires your ingredient to be rolled like a cigar and sliced. The ingredient remains rolled while you slice. This method helps retain as much flavor as possible before adding to your dish.

SLICE

This technique requires you to use your chef's knife to cut your ingredient into thin, equal parts with a smooth, swift, downward motion.

Chiffonade

Julienne

Slice

BASIC COOKING TECHNIQUES

This section contains a few of the most commonly used cooking techniques. It's important to know that baking isn't the same as roasting. If you watch cooking shows you'll hear the word *purée* about a gazillion times, but they never really explain what that is. You may already know some of these techniques, even if you don't know the technical terms. (You're such a natural!)

BOIL VS. SIMMER

The technical differences between boiling and simmering start with temperature. Boiling requires a minimum temperature of 212 degrees Fahrenheit while simmering requires a minimum of about 190 degrees Fahrenheit. Now, I know you're not going to be taking the temperature of your water, so here are some visual cues to help you distinguish between the two:

- **Simmer:** characterized by smaller bubbles in the liquid and less vapor rising from the water. Simmering is good for braising and reducing sauces. It's a gentler cooking method than boiling. This is important, because it can help ingredients build a depth of flavor over time without burning.
- **Boiling:** characterized by large, rolling bubbles and larger, more visible wafts of vapor. Boiling is good for quickly breaking down ingredients and bringing them to the right temperature. However, boiling is not a useful method for long periods of time.

REDUCE

Reducing is the term used to describe thickening a liquid and enhancing the flavor. This method is most commonly used for sauces and when adding wine to dishes.

BRAISE

Braising is a two-part method:

1. Sear the meat in a pan with a fat source, like butter or oil.
2. Add liquid and bring to a slow simmer for long periods of time.

My favorite method is called brown braising:

- Sear the meat in a pan with a fat source.
- Remove the meat and set it aside.
- In the same pan, add some vegetables and aromatics (ingredients that add to or deepen the flavor of the dish—ginger, garlic, or herbs like allspice and rosemary), releasing their flavors into the pan for a few minutes.
- Pour in a liquid, either wine or stock (or some combination of the two), and stir, scraping the bottom of the pan to incorporate any browned bits (see the Deglaze section on page 11). The brown bits are full of flavor and add delicious depth to the dish.
- Place the meat back into the pan and add more liquid, either stock or water. Cover and let simmer for at least three hours.

SAUTÉ

Sautéing usually involves cooking ingredients over high heat with a little bit of fat (like oils or butter) over a short period of time.

ROAST VS. BAKE

Much like boiling and simmering, the difference between roasting and baking is generally distinguished by temperature.

- **Roast:** temperatures are typically 400 degrees Fahrenheit and higher. This method is commonly associated with heartier vegetables that benefit from the browning process at a higher temperature.

- **Bake:** temperatures are typically lower than 400 degrees Fahrenheit. Another distinguishing factor is the ingredients used in the dish. Baking is a gentler method used for baked goods and more temperamental meats.

> **Pro tip:** Baking and roasting can be done together. Start with roasting to get great color and texture, then follow it up by baking and bring the food to temp without overcooking.

POACH

Poaching is a method in which an ingredient is simmered in a small amount of liquid. For instance, butter poaching refers to simmering an ingredient in a pan of melted butter. Another example is poached eggs, or raw eggs simmered in a small amount of water or stock.

PANFRY VS. DEEP-FRY

The difference between panfrying and deep-frying is the amount of oil used.

- **Panfry:** requires less oil and does not completely submerge the ingredient.
- **Deep-fry:** requires large amounts of oil, and the ingredient is submerged, as with fries. Although it uses more oil, deep-frying requires less cooking time.

Both panfrying and deep-frying are valuable techniques that can bring a crisp and flavorful finish to various dishes.

DEGLAZE

Deglazing is typically done after sautéing to loosen the browned bits stuck to the bottom of the pan and incorporate them into the liquid. This technique creates a greater depth of flavor to the dish. To deglaze a pan, keep the heat high, remove any meats from the pan, and add some liquid to the pan (pasta water, wine, beer, apple cider vinegar, and juice are good examples). As the liquid bubbles, scrape the bottom of the pan to loosen the bits that are stuck to the bottom. Stir to incorporate those flavorful bits into the liquid, and let it reduce a bit to enhance the flavor. Deglazing can be used while braising or making soups and sauces.

PURÉE

Puréeing involves cooking vegetables, fruits, or legumes and then blending them, typically with a fat or liquid, to create a smooth, flavorful sauce. Purées can be used to thicken soups and sauces or to decorate your plate with a flavor-balancing ingredient.

BASIC RATIOS

Cooking requires a bit of math. (Don't worry! There's no math test.) You should put certain ratios in your mental file to make cooking an easier, more enjoyable experience. Once you have these ratios memorized (or not—I mean, you bought this book, so feel free to have it out as a reference whenever you cook), you can use them for recipes seamlessly and fearlessly.

P.S. You're more likely to cook from home if you feel like you know what you're doing.

RICE RATIOS

There are many different types of rice with different liquid to rice ratios.

Following is a list of the most popular rice types with the ratios needed to serve four people. Each type of rice is cooked the same way: bring the liquid and rice to a boil together, and then reduce to a simmer until the liquid is absorbed.

- **White rice ratio:** 2 cups water to 1 cup rice, cooked for 15–20 minutes.
- **Basmati rice:** 1½ cups water to 1 cup rice,

cooked for 15–20 minutes. Most commonly served with Indian food.

- **Wild rice:** 3 cups water to 1 cup rice, cooked for 50–60 minutes. (Despite its name, wild rice is not actually rice. It's the grains of four different species of grass.) Most commonly used as a white rice substitute.
- **Jasmine rice:** 2 cups water to 1 cup rice, cooked for 15–20 minutes. Most commonly served with Thai food.
- **Brown rice:** 2 cups water to 1 cup rice, cooked for 35–45 minutes. Most commonly used as a healthier alternative to white rice.
- **Arborio rice:** 2½ cups water to 1 cup rice, cooked for about 20 minutes. Most commonly served as risotto.

PICKLING RATIOS

Cucumbers aren't the only thing that can be pickled, baby. Let's talk about it. Pickling is the process of boiling water with vinegar and adding that mixture to a jar of veggies (think onions, peppers, and green beans). The jar is then covered and refrigerated, typically for at least a day, to let science get its science on. The result is a pickled veggie of your choice.

CLASSIC PICKLE RECIPE

1 cup water
1 cup vinegar
1 tablespoon sugar
½–1 tablespoon salt

DIRECTIONS:

1. Combine water, vinegar, sugar, and salt in a small saucepan. Bring to a boil on the stove top over high heat.
2. While waiting for the water mixture to come to a boil, place your preferred veggies and spices in a 16-ounce mason jar.
3. Pour the boiling water over the veggies in the jar and seal.
4. Leave the jar out to rest for one hour and then place the jar in the refrigerator for at least 24 hours.

Feel free to incorporate hot peppers, shallots, saffron, or other spices to add your personal flare.

Pro tip: The longer you let the pickled veggies sit, the better they will taste—preferably 72 hours.

ROUX RATIOS

No, unfortunately we're not talking about that dope girl from HBO's show *Euphoria*. (Shoutout to Zendaya! I will make roux for you anytime.) What is it, then? A roux is a building block for most sauces. It consists of equal parts fat and flour *by weight*. You can use a kitchen scale to make sure your parts are equal. If you don't have a scale, a safe ratio would be ½ cup fat, like butter or oil, with ¾ to 1 cup flour.

ROUX INSTRUCTIONS

1. Put your fat source in a pan over medium to high heat.
2. Once the fat starts to thin and bubble, add the flour a little bit at a time, stirring with each combination. This will create a sauce that ranges in consistency from thick, like cake frosting, to thin, like soup.
3. The length of time used to cook the roux and the color once finished determines its name and uses.

WHITE ROUX:

Cook time: about 5 minutes

Color: pale, just slightly darker than when first combined

Consistency: This roux is slightly thick, think cake batter.

This roux has a shallow depth of flavor and is most commonly used as a thickening agent for white sauces like Alfredo.

BLONDE ROUX:

Cook time: about 15 minutes

Color: tan

Consistency: Slightly thinner than white roux. Closer in texture to applesauce.

Blonde roux is most commonly used for gravy. It has a mild but distinguishable flavor.

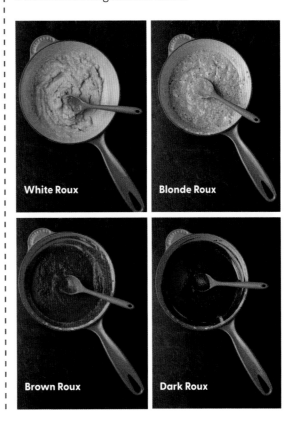

White Roux

Blonde Roux

Brown Roux

Dark Roux

BROWN ROUX:

Cook time: 25 to 30 minutes

Color: light brown, like peanut butter

Consistency: Even thinner than blonde roux. This roux is closest in consistency to tomato soup.

Brown roux yields a rich, nutty flavor. It's commonly used to add flavor to stews.

DARK ROUX:

Cook time: about 45 to 50 minutes

Color: rich brown, like chocolate (sometimes called chocolate roux because of its color)

Consistency: Very thin, like water

Dark roux has the richest flavor. This roux is most commonly used in Creole dishes like jambalaya and gumbo.

The Road to Right Now

Excuse me if I get emotional writing this. It has truly been a journey. This section, "The Road to Right Now," is an accumulation of some of the recipes that catapulted me to where I am today.

My dear friend Maryann sent me a flyer one morning telling me to apply to be on Fox's TV competition *MasterChef*. I loved to cook, and loved the show, but I never ever thought my two minutes of spontaneous boldness would lead to all of this.

My time on that show was challenging. I was six weeks pregnant with my third child upon arriving in Los Angeles, and morning sickness took full effect as soon as I stepped into that amazing kitchen. I was stressed every day, trying to impress the very chefs I had been watching and studying my entire life. I heard voices in my head constantly telling me, "You're not good enough. You're not worthy. You won't win anyway. You're just here to help fill a demographic." Those thoughts were difficult to silence, and even more difficult not to believe.

Audition after audition, interview after interview, I kept making it through to the next round. When I got that apron, I became a member of a new family of chefs that brought me comfort and support, which ultimately led me to the Row House Publishing team. My Row House team helped me bring this book to you. And all because I said *yes* to being uncomfortable and pushing past my fears, and *no* to doubting myself.

I have switched up the recipes a bit. They're inspired by the original recipes I created in the *MasterChef* kitchen but reformulated for user convenience and flavor. Thank you to the people who believed in me, and a huge thanks to you for buying this book. I'm grateful that my recipes stood out among the crowd of chef hopefuls. Those recipes led me here, walking with gratitude on The Road to Right Now.

CHAPTER ONE

RECIPES FROM MY HEART TO YOUR HOME

This section represents the timeline of my MasterChef journey, from my first audition to my last competitive cook. Despite these being the recipes that got me on television and propelled my culinary career, I promise they are still beginner- and budget-friendly! Every once in a while, I whip up one of these to reminisce on a very special time in my life, and I hope you can feel the same joy when you prepare them for yourself and the people you love. Happy Cooking, friends!

MAMA'S ZUPPA TOSCANO

After I sent my video audition for *MasterChef*, I was invited to a banquet hall in Chicago to present my first dish. It had to be cooked ahead of time so it could be assembled at the location in about three minutes. I stressed for a whole week, trying to figure out what to make. It needed to be bold enough to stand out, but without warmers. I was terrified of bringing the judges a cold dish that tasted best when warm. While the judges are trained to taste the greatness of a once-hot plate, even after it's cooled down, I was not satisfied. My food needed to be warm, but how?

I decided to make soup. My mom makes a special soup for us all the time, and it is, without a doubt, my favorite dish of hers. I stayed up all night testing different methods: some made with wine, some without, some with egg drop, others topped with grated Parmesan. In the end, I settled on a recipe similar to this one. I placed my flavorful concoction in a thermos to keep it warm and made the 45-minute drive to the city with my husband (and biggest fan). I served it in a homemade bread bowl with a purple potato purée decorating the plate. Looking back, I hate how I plated that dish, but I loved how it tasted, and clearly they did as well. Here's my new and improved version of Mama's Zuppa Toscano soup.

PREP TIME: 10 MINUTES ❤ **COOK TIME:** 1 HOUR ❤ **SERVES:** 4–8

INGREDIENTS:

16 ounces Italian sausage

2 medium white onions, diced

¼ cup dry white wine

6 cups chicken broth

5 medium potatoes

3 cups packed kale, precut and washed

2 cups heavy cream

1 teaspoon Italian seasoning

1 teaspoon garlic powder

1 teaspoon onion powder

2 eggs, beaten

¼ cup grated Parmesan or pecorino Romano cheese

Bread (for serving)

> **Flashback:** I remember frantically trying different ways to elevate this soup and making my parents and husband taste each version. They clearly chose a winner!

DIRECTIONS:

1. Brown and crumble the sausage in a stock pot over medium-high heat.

2. Transfer to a plate and set aside.

3. In the same pot, add the onions and cook for about 5 minutes, or until slightly soft and translucent.

4. Deglaze the pot with the wine and cook for an additional 5 minutes to cook out the alcohol. Stir constantly to remove the bits that are stuck to the bottom of the pan and to prevent anything from burning.

5. Add the broth and potatoes and boil until the potatoes are al dente (cooked but firm). This should take about 15 minutes.

6. Once the potatoes can be easily punctured, but not so soft that they fall off the knife, add the kale.

7. Cook the kale for 7 minutes, at which point the potatoes should be soft.

8. Add the cream and seasonings.

9. Bring to a simmer and gently pour in the eggs, stirring constantly. The soup will be hot enough to cook the egg drop.

10. Remove from the heat and fold in the cheese.

11. Serve warm with bread.

TAVIA'S CUPCAKES
(SWEET POTATO CUPCAKES)

In preparation for the show, I wanted to brush up on my baking skills. Actually, I needed to *acquire* some baking skills because I had next to none. I could hear Gordon Ramsay in my head saying, "Lexy! Bloody hell, why would you come to *MasterChef* if you don't know how to bake?" Just typing that gave me chills. He is, without a doubt, the most intimidating and oddly comforting man I've ever met. Anyway, I needed a crash course in baking—and fast. I hit up my sister and she agreed to help me create a recipe guaranteed to wow the judges. I never made this recipe on the show, but it gave me the confidence I needed to excel in the baking challenge. Thank you so much, Latavia. I hope this recipe brings you joy.

PREP TIME: 20 MINUTES ❤ **COOK TIME:** 10 MINUTES ❤ **YIELD:** 12 CUPCAKES

INGREDIENTS:

2 sweet potatoes, peeled and sliced

6 cups water

2¾ cups flour

1 tablespoon baking powder

2 teaspoons ground cinnamon

1 teaspoon salt

1 teaspoon ground nutmeg

⅓ cup butter, softened

1½ cups brown sugar

¾ cup almond milk or milk of choice

2 eggs

1 teaspoon vanilla extract

Frosting of your choice (optional)

DIRECTIONS:

1. Preheat the oven to 350°F. Line 12 cups of a muffin pan.
2. Boil the sweet potato in a medium pot for 10 minutes, or until soft. The thinner your slices, the quicker your potatoes will cook.
3. Mix the flour, baking powder, cinnamon, salt, and nutmeg in a bowl.
4. In a separate, larger bowl, beat the butter and sugar until smooth.
5. Add the milk, eggs, and vanilla extract. Beat until well combined.
6. Slowly mix the dry ingredients (flour mixture) with the wet ingredients (milk and egg mixture). The batter should be fairly thick but not stiff.
7. When the sweet potatoes are done, drain the water and either beat them or blend them until smooth.
8. Add 1 cup of the sweet potato purée to the batter and fold to combine.
9. Scoop the batter into the prepared muffin pan. Be careful to not fill the liners to the top or they will overflow; fill each ¾ of the way to ensure proper baking.
10. Bake in the oven for 10 minutes, or until the tops are golden brown and a knife dipped in the center comes out clean.
11. Cool completely before topping with frosting, if using.

Pro tip: Additional purée can be sweetened with brown sugar to taste and eaten with leftovers, used as baby/toddler food, or saved to use for more of these delicious cupcakes! Purée will hold in the fridge for up to one week.

Flashback: We didn't even run to the store to create this recipe. My girl looked through her kitchen, took out her notebook, and helped me whip up something I could have easily shared with the *MasterChef* judges.

APRON-WORTHY BURGER
(AKA AUDITION DISH)

My audition dish was inspired by my best friend, Makaehla.. She introduced me to what I considered to be luxury ingredients. She showed me things like prosciutto, charcuterie boards, goat cheese—stuff I couldn't even pronounce before I met her. As it turns out, that stuff monumentally changed my life. But I was also inspired by my favorite cartoon, *Bob's Burgers*. I needed to present something different to the *MasterChef* judges. I didn't want to give them a dish that wasn't me. I knew my competitors would be making dishes with knockout ingredients, like rack of lamb and risotto. While those were impressive meals to serve, they weren't a part of my life. So instead, I came up with a black garlic burger, stuffed with tomato basil goat cheese, and a side of honey goat cheese brussels sprouts. It was a burger elevated enough to get me a hug, a smile, and an apron from the one and only Chef Gordon Ramsay.

PREP TIME: 10 MINUTES ♥ **COOK TIME:** 10 MINUTES ♥ **YIELD:** 5 BURGERS

INGREDIENTS:

2 pounds ground beef

2 tablespoons crushed black garlic

2 tablespoons salt

1 tablespoon ground black pepper

1 tablespoon minced garlic

1 tablespoon freeze-dried chives

1 egg

4 ounces plain goat cheese

2 tablespoons basil chiffonade

2 tablespoons chopped sun-dried tomatoes

1 teaspoon red pepper flakes

5 slices pepper Jack cheese

½ cup mayonnaise

½ tablespoon Creole seasoning*

5 brioche buns

5 crisp lettuce leaves

5 tomato slices

1 red onion, sliced

* **Note:** I like to use Tony Chachere's Creole Seasoning.

DIRECTIONS:

1. With gloved hands, mix the ground beef with the black garlic, salt, pepper, and minced garlic until well combined.

2. Crack the egg directly into a bowl and add the burger meat, mixing with gloved hands until fully incorporated.

3. Add the chives and mix once more.

4. In a separate bowl, crush the goat cheese with a fork. Add the basil, sun-dried tomatoes, and pepper flakes and mix with a fork until smooth.

5. Remove three-quarters of the burger meat and separate into five balls on a baking sheet. Flatten each burger ball into a patty, cupping the edges to form a bowl-like shape. The patties should not exceed ¼ inch in thickness.

6. Scoop a spoonful of goat cheese into the center of each bowl-like patty.

7. Separate the remaining burger meat into five chunks and flatten to about ¼ inch thick. Lay these on top of each bowl-like patty. Using your pointer finger and thumb, pinch around the edges of each patty, enclosing the goat cheese mixture.

8. Place the patties, top side down, on a griddle or skillet and cook over medium heat for 5 minutes undisturbed.

9. Flip the patties over and lay a slice of pepper Jack cheese on each patty. Cook for 2–3 minutes, until the patties are cooked through and the goat cheese is melted.

10. In a small bowl, combine the mayonnaise and Creole seasoning and spread on the underside of the top brioche bun.

11. On the bottom bun, layer the lettuce, tomato, and red onion. Place the fully cooked burgers on top of the veggies and place the sauced bun on top.

Flashback: This was not my originally planned audition dish—the Sweet Potato Cupcakes were. But after racking my brain to figure out what my motivation for the dish would be, I decided to change it. I didn't want to be labeled as a baker when baking was not my strong suit.

HOT LAVA CAKE

"Why was she put in the top three?" "That molten lava cake looked disgusting." "This is not complex at all. My seventeen-year-old daughter makes this all the time." These are just a few of the hate comments about me the second I showed some promise on *MasterChef*. I'll respond to those now. I was in the top three because the judges selected my dish. I'm sorry you didn't approve of my cake, but not really, because Chef Ramsay loved it. Not every gourmet dish needs to be complex. If you've ever had a hater who wished they were the player, I get it. Make this cake with me and let the positive vibes flow like the chocolate lava tucked inside this decadent dessert. Serve it with ice cream or berries.

PREP TIME: 10 MINUTES ♥ **COOK TIME:** 10 MINUTES ♥ **SERVES:** 5

INGREDIENTS:

¼ cup butter

¼ cup semi-sweet chocolate chips

¼ cup bittersweet chocolate (80% cacao or higher)

¼ cup granulated sugar

3 eggs

1 teaspoon vanilla extract

¼ cup flour

Nonstick baking spray

DIRECTIONS:

1. Preheat the oven to 400°F.
2. Melt the butter in a medium glass or microwave-safe bowl. Heat in the microwave for 30 seconds.
3. Immediately mix both semi-sweet and dark chocolate with the melted butter until the chocolate is melted and combined.
4. Add the sugar and stir until combined, about 1 minute.
5. Crack the eggs into the bowl and beat thoroughly, about 3 minutes.
6. Add the vanilla and stir to combine.
7. Once the egg is fully combined, fold in the flour.
8. Spray 5 small ramekins or the wells of a cupcake tin with nonstick baking spray.* Divide the batter among the 5 ramekins or cupcake wells.
9. Bake in the oven for 10 minutes, or until the edges have begun to pull away from the sides of the ramekins and the centers are still jiggly.
10. Flip upside down to remove from the pan and serve immediately.

* **Note:** You can sprinkle the baking dish with cocoa or espresso powder for a little extra kick.

Flashback: I ruined this dish the first time I made it and had to scrap the whole thing and start over. I thought I would be going home, but instead ended up in the top three!

ELEVATED PHILLY CHEESESTEAK

This dish still haunts me. I know that sounds weird, but let me explain. I made this dish for a personal legend, the great Roy Choi. If you don't know who he is, please pause and look him up. The dude is freaking amazing. Anyway, he loved this dish and told me to cook with confidence. Those words pierced my soul. Roy basically told me to silence my self-doubt and negativity, without him even knowing they were there. I still struggle to do this, but I'll start therapy when I'm through writing this recipe.

Regardless, I cooked a near-perfect dish for Roy. It's an elevated version of my favorite street food (see page 89 for the Not-from-Philly Cheesesteak). But I broke the dog on cheese sauce! It was a mistake that cost me immunity and ultimately sealed my fate on *MasterChef*. I've tweaked some things so you can nail this dish every single time. With the improvements I made to this recipe, I'm convinced that Roy Choi would love the heck out of this cheese sauce. Cook this one with confidence for me. Your success is inspiring.

PREP TIME: 5 MINUTES ♥ **COOK TIME:** 30 MINUTES ♥ **SERVES:** 2

INGREDIENTS:

2 ribeye steaks

2 teaspoons salt

2 teaspoons ground black pepper

1 teaspoon grapeseed oil

4 tablespoons butter

4 ounces (½ cup) sliced baby bella mushrooms

1 green pepper, sliced

½ white onion, sliced

2 tablespoons flour

1 cup heavy cream

½ teaspoon cayenne pepper

½ teaspoon paprika

1 cup shredded pepper Jack cheese

DIRECTIONS:

1. Preheat the oven to 350°F.
2. Heat a cast iron skillet over high heat for about 3 minutes.
3. Season the steaks with the salt and pepper.
4. Drizzle the oil into the pan.
5. Sear the steaks in the skillet for 3 minutes.*
6. Flip and sear on the other side for an additional 3 minutes.
7. Top each steak with 1 tablespoon butter and place in the oven for 5 minutes.
8. Take the skillet out of the oven, remove the steaks from the skillet, and set on a plate or cutting board to rest.
9. Using the same skillet, cook the mushrooms, green pepper, and onion over medium-high heat for 7–10 minutes, until tender.
10. In a small saucepan, melt the remaining 2 tablespoons butter and whisk with the flour.
11. Cook until foaming and add the cream.
12. Cook for 5 minutes or until slightly thickened.
13. Add the seasonings and cheese and stir until combined.
14. To plate, cover one half of the plate with cheese sauce and place a steak in the center. One half of the steak should cover the cheese.
15. Top with the veggies and serve immediately.

* **Note:** To learn how to prepare and cook the perfect ribeye steak, see page 151 in the "Dinner's Ready!" section.

Flashback: I don't think this was shown on TV, but Gordon told me that if my sauce had been perfect, this dish would've won. That win would've granted me immunity—immunity from the very dish that sent me home.

FOOD FOR YOUR SOUL (SOUL FOOD)

Corn bread, collard greens, and sweet potato pie
Little pieces of peace my heart just can't deny
When I was told to cook from the depths of my soul
A meal full of history was the only route I could go
Soul food has a feeling, a power that won't budge
From the hands of those that raised us, we sum it up
    as love
It was that love that got me started

That love that gave me this chance
That love to which I departed
That love in which I stand
That love that gave me this opportunity
To make my way to you
And with that love I bring you this recipe
Send me home to sweet soul food.

Soul food is more than just food from the South. Its origins are rooted in people hoping to preserve a legacy by passing down recipes to their descendants. Every bite symbolizes tradition and was birthed from necessity and strengthened with love. That's what my grandma gave me, and her mother gave to her, and so on. So when I was given the challenge of cooking a dish from my greatest inspiration, there really wasn't a question in my mind. I give all my love when I make this dish, and those I share it with fill me up too. This recipe might have been the end of my time in the *MasterChef* kitchen, but it was the birth of a brand-new opportunity: an opportunity to pass my heart to your home.

BEFORE YOU BEGIN:

The key to good soul food starts before you put anything in the oven or on the stove. An organized game plan is key to any great dish but especially with this recipe.

To ensure everything is ready around the same time, start with prepping your food. Following the steps in order will reduce the amount of time some things are done before others.

Start the greens at least two hours before you want to eat.

Peel and cube the sweet potatoes. Set them aside on a baking sheet.

The chicken should soak in the fridge for 30 minutes before it's ready to be fried.

PREP TIME: 40 MINUTES ❤ **COOK TIME:** 1.5 HOURS ❤ **SERVES:** 6–8

INGREDIENTS:
COLLARD GREENS

3 tablespoons butter

2 tablespoons minced garlic

8 cups shredded collard greens, packed

6 cups chicken broth

FRIED CHICKEN

3 pounds chicken tenders

3 cups buttermilk

1 cup Buffalo sauce

5 cups flour

1 tablespoon onion powder

1 tablespoon garlic powder

2 teaspoons paprika

4 tablespoons seasoned salt

8 cups canola oil

SWEET POTATOES

4 sweet potatoes, peeled and cubed

5 tablespoons plus 1 teaspoon butter

⅓ cup brown sugar

1½ teaspoons ground cinnamon

Recipe Continues

DIRECTIONS:

FOR THE COLLARD GREENS:

1. Melt the butter in a large pot over medium-low heat.
2. Add the garlic to the melted butter. Cook over medium-low heat for 2 minutes.
3. Add the greens and chicken broth. Cover and cook for 1½ to 2 hours.

FOR THE FRIED CHICKEN:

1. Soak the chicken tenders in a bowl of the buttermilk and Buffalo sauce. Chill in the fridge for 30 minutes.
2. In a separate bowl, combine the flour, onion powder, garlic powder, paprika, and seasoned salt. If your flour does not visibly look seasoned, it is not seasoned enough.
3. After 30 minutes to 1 hour, remove the chicken from the fridge and dredge in the flour, shaking off any excess.
4. Heat the oil in an aluminum pot over high heat. (See pro tip.)
5. Once hot enough, gently place the chicken in the grease and cook for 6 minutes. The chicken should be golden brown and crispy.
6. Place the chicken on plate lined with paper towels to drain excess grease.

FOR THE SWEET POTATOES:

1. Preheat the oven to 350°F. Place the sweet potato cubes on a baking sheet.
2. Melt the butter in the microwave in a microwave-safe bowl, or on the stovetop in a small saucepan over medium-low heat for 30 seconds.
3. Mix the sugar and cinnamon into the melted butter and pour the mixture over the sweet potatoes.
4. Bake in the oven for 25–30 minutes, until the sweet potatoes are tender.

PUT IT ALL TOGETHER:

After my grandma was done cooking, she would sit in her chair, cross her legs, and let us all know the food was ready as she leaned back to rest. We would gratefully get up, grab a plate, and load up on as much food as we wanted. If you tackle this meal, I advise you to do the same thing.

Pro tip: To see if your oil is hot enough, place the end of a wooden spoon in the grease; if it bubbles, your oil is ready. If you don't have a wooden spoon, sprinkle some of the seasoned flour into the grease. If the flour bubbles and crackles, your oil is ready.

Flashback: I told myself I wouldn't cry if I got eliminated—a lie. I had so much I wanted to say but was overcome by emotion. I felt like I let down the ones I was trying to honor the most. Looking back over my time in that kitchen, I have many wonderful memories. I made friends, had an amazing time, and learned how to live in the now. I have no regrets. This was one of the most incredible times in my life. Thank you for letting me share it with you.

Mama Needs a Break . . . and Fast!

I can hear my grandma now, giving thanks to God for another day. It truly is a blessing to wake up with breath in your lungs, a roof over your head, and my favorite, breakfast! I'll be honest: Most nights are not restful for me. My youngest is still nursing and reminds me of it constantly. My oldest child is working through potty training and, well, some nights are easier than others. My firstborn daughter crawls out of her bed every night, and while at first I enjoy some sweet snuggles, she eventually turns into a grandfather clock, spinning and kicking with each passing hour. All that to say, breakfast is a must if I am to awaken from my zombie-like trance in the morning. I give my tired body whatever it demands, sweet or savory.

This breakfast section has three equally valuable parts:

1. Spectacular Smoothies, for the Shay Mitchell in us (I'll explain later).
2. Eggtastic Breakfasts, because eggs are literally the first thing that comes to mind when I hear the word *breakfast*.
3. The Sweet Side of the Bread, or baked goods, for the sweeter mornings.

The best part about breakfast is putting meaningful fuel in your body that feels (and tastes) good. These recipes can stand alone. Or they can be paired with any other recipe in the breakfast section. It's all up to you. Consider yourself the king or queen of breakfast! Adjust your crown and get cooking.

CHAPTER TWO

SPECTACULAR SMOOTHIES

I heard Shay Mitchell say that she prefers to drink her calories in the morning. She believes it gives her stomach a warmup before she bogs it down with a whole meal. This inspired me, so I tried to drink my calories too. My stomach laughed in my face and grumbled, "Girl, if you don't feed me like you know me. . . ." Still, on those days when I'm feeling light and whimsical, or if I just want a snack while making my actual breakfast, I whip up one of these spectacular smoothies.

BLACK AND BLUEBERRY PEACH SMOOTHIE

The inspiration for this recipe came from one of my favorite sandwich shops. While I love the food at this little sandwich shop, I couldn't believe the prices! Why was this little gem of a smoothie $7? Excuse me, ma'am. No way was I going to let them get away with that (again). So, I sipped on my overpriced, tiny smoothie and dreamed up this quirky little darling, which can be made for a fraction of the restaurant price (it's quick too). My Black and Blueberry Peach Smoothie is a refreshing breakfast that's easy to make and definitely a summer favorite. Tell that pricey smoothie shop that they won't be getting your $7 anytime soon.

PREP TIME: 2 MINUTES (TOLD YOU IT WAS QUICK!) ❤ **PROCESSING TIME:** 1 MINUTE ❤ **SERVES:** 2–4

INGREDIENTS:

$\frac{1}{2}$ cup frozen blueberries

$\frac{1}{2}$ cup frozen blackberries

$\frac{1}{2}$ cup frozen peaches

$\frac{1}{2}$ cup almond milk or milk of choice

$1\frac{1}{2}$ cups peach nectar*

A few fresh berries (for garnish, optional)

* **Note:** Peach nectar can usually be found in the international foods or fruit juice aisles, usually labeled "Jumex."

DIRECTIONS:

1. Combine the blueberries, blackberries, peaches, milk, and peach nectar in a high-speed blender.
2. Blend for 1 minute or until smooth. Pour into glasses, garnish with fresh berries if desired, and serve.

Pro tip: You can absolutely swap any of the frozen fruits with fresh fruits and add $\frac{1}{4}$ cup ice for every 1 cup frozen fruit.

CREAMY MATCHA SMOOTHIE

When did I fall in love with matcha? Now. I fell in love right now. Matcha is one of those "I can't believe I haven't been using this my whole life" kind of ingredients. I usually stay true to my background with the recipes in this book, except for this one here. This smoothie is semisweet, without losing that bold matcha flavor. It tastes like a piña colada on steroids. It's also full of nutritional benefits. Matcha is believed to improve brain function and aid in weight loss. Since matcha is a type of green tea, it packs a powerful energy boost, making this smoothie the perfect kick start to your morning routine.

PREP TIME: 2 MINUTES (NOT MATCHA TIME AT ALL!) ♥ **PROCESSING TIME:** 1 MINUTE ♥ **SERVES:** 2–4

INGREDIENTS:

1 cup ice

1 cup almond milk or milk of choice

½ cup vanilla yogurt*

1 teaspoon shredded coconut (sweetened or unsweetened), plus more for garnish (optional)

1 teaspoon matcha

2 teaspoons honey

* **Substitution:** Yogurt can be substituted with Greek yogurt or other flavor variations for a fun twist.

DIRECTIONS:

1. Combine the ice, milk, yogurt, coconut, matcha, and honey in a high-speed blender.

2. Blend for 1 minute or until smooth. Pour into glasses, sprinkle with more coconut if desired, and serve.

Pro tip: Try making this recipe ahead of time and freezing each serving for an even faster morning routine.

BAHAMA MAMA BREEZE TROPICAL FRUIT SMOOTHIE

I've never been to the Bahamas, but it's easy to pretend when I'm sipping on this island-inspired smoothie. If you're someone who likes the sweeter things in life, you'll love this tart, dessert-like smoothie. It's a perfect blend of classic island fruits and fruit juices. This beauty is full of tropical flavor that the whole family will love. Mine sure does!

PREP TIME: 2 MINUTES ♥ **PROCESSING TIME:** 1 MINUTE ♥ **SERVES:** 2–4

INGREDIENTS:

2 cups mixed frozen fruit, such as peaches, strawberries, mango, and pineapple*

1 cup pineapple juice

1 cup orange juice

½ cup plain yogurt

Fresh fruit (for garnish, optional)

* **Note:** Walmart has a tropical medley blend that works fantastic in this recipe. Otherwise, buying bags of each frozen ingredient and combining them in a gallon-sized zip-top storage bag is a great way to create a medley on your own.

DIRECTIONS:

1. Combine the frozen fruit, pineapple juice, orange juice, and yogurt in a high-speed blender.
2. Blend until smooth, about 1 minute. Pour into glasses, garnish with fresh fruit if desired, and serve.

THE GREEN SMOOTHIE

Green smoothies—either you love them or you hate them. Unless it's this one, then you either love it or you love it more. I've always struggled to fit veggies into my diet, so this smoothie has worked wonders for me. It's sweet enough, easy enough, and nutritious enough for those who are veggie-challenged, like me. Maybe it's the placebo effect of knowing that I'm consuming something that's good for me, but my mirrors always seem a little kinder to me after I drink this smoothie. (Joking, I'm joking. But also kinda serious? How about you try it and let me know?)

PREP TIME: 1 MINUTE ❤ **PROCESSING TIME:** 1 MINUTE ❤ **SERVES:** 2–4

INGREDIENTS:

2 cups spinach, packed

2 cups vanilla almond milk or milk of choice

1 frozen banana

DIRECTIONS:

1. Combine the spinach, milk, and banana in a high-speed blender.

2. Blend until smooth, about 1 minute. Pour into glasses and serve.

CHAPTER THREE

EGGTASTIC BREAKFASTS

As a stay-at-home parent, and someone who prides herself on cooking marvelous meals with what some would call pocket change, breakfast time just screams eggs! They're cheap, quick to make, and incredibly delicious when prepared the right way. Honestly, nothing will make me leave a breakfast establishment faster than poorly cooked eggs. This oval-shaped beauty can be the star of the show, or a clever companion. In this section, you'll find a little bit of both. So skip the bland and uninspired foods you grab on your way to work. Put together your outfit the day before, if need be, and use those extra twenty minutes to make a breakfast your taste buds deserve.

THE PERFECT EGG 5 WAYS

The pleats in a chef hat are said to symbolize one hundred ways to prepare an egg. One day, I plan to learn them all. Until then, these are my five favorite ways to cook an egg. These techniques don't discriminate between a six-dollar carton of eggs and an eighty-eight-cent carton of eggs. That's what I love about them. Give a man a fish and he eats for a day; teach a man to fish and he eats for life. That was my poetic attempt at telling you, "We gon' learn to cook some eggs today, baby!"

POACHED

To cook a flawless poached egg, there are a few rules to follow:

Rule #1: *Never* salt the water. Putting vinegar in the water helps the egg stay together and form that beautiful dome-like shape. Salt will hinder the coagulation process. It breaks up the bonds in the egg, leaving you with a pot full of white wisps.

Rule #2: Get the right ratios. You should add about ½ to 1 full tablespoon of vinegar per cup of water. The water line should hit the middle of the saucepan. For my pan, the ratio looks like this: 5 cups of water to 5 tablespoons of vinegar.

Rule #3: Strain the egg. I like a clean-looking poached egg, so I strain any loose egg whites. To do this, place a small metal sieve over the top of a cup that has an opening large enough to hold the sieve in place. Crack the egg in the sieve and let it sit for a few seconds.

Rule #4: Heat the water, but not too much. Your water should be hot enough that you can see small bubbles at the bottom and sides of the pan but not so hot that it's rapidly boiling.

Rule #5: Create a vortex. Using a whisk or spoon, swirl a vortex in the center of the pan by aggressively stirring in a circular motion. The vortex you create should be about 2 inches in diameter. Once the vortex is formed and you can clearly see the bottom of the pan, take the sieve and dump the egg in the center of the vortex.

Rule #6: Timing is everything. Cook the egg for 4–5 minutes. The egg should be completely white and floating slightly above the bottom of the pan. The closer the egg floats to the top of the water, the more cooked the yolk will be. Remove the egg from the pan using a slotted spoon, and place on a plate lined with paper towel to drain any excess water before plating.

SCRAMBLED

Don't let this simple dish fool you. It's not as simple as you think. I guarantee every person reading this has tasted an overcooked scrambled egg. Let's break this down:

- At no point whatsoever should your eggs be browned.
- Don't be afraid of a little moisture. They're eggs, not bagels.
- You salt your eggs before you cook them, don't you? I knew it. It's okay. I used to do that too, but I was wrong!
- Use a nonstick pan. If you don't have one, buy one. It may be your greatest investment to date. If you don't use a nonstick pan, the eggs will stick to the sides and bottoms of the pan, and you will either burn them or ruin them by combining the brown stuff in with the rest of the mixture.

Pro tip: If you'd like to add peppers or other veggies, sauté them first and then add your eggs (see below).

Directions for scrumptious scrambled eggs:

1. In a nonstick pan over low to medium heat, add 1 tablespoon of butter for every two eggs you're cooking.
2. Once the butter is melted, crack your eggs into the pan.
3. Using a rubber scraper, press down on the yolks to pop them and then stir rapidly to combine the yolks with the whites until the mixture is mostly yellow.
4. Once your eggs have been combined, reduce the heat to the lowest setting and stir constantly until the eggs begin to form but still look fairly moist.
5. Add ¼ teaspoon salt and a pinch of black pepper per two eggs cooked.
6. Remove the pan from the heat and continue to fold the mixture into itself by scraping the edges and dragging them to the center until the egg is formed with just enough moisture to leave a small streak in the pan.

Additions: I love to eat my scrambled eggs with a few shaved mini peppers, one stalk of fresh chopped green onion, and a dollop of cream cheese:

1. Cook the peppers in a skillet for 2 minutes, then add your eggs. Once the eggs have been combined, add a spoonful of cream cheese and continue with the directions above.
2. Top with green onions and add a side of your favorite toast.

For a perfect hard-boiled egg:

1. Place the egg at the bottom of a pot and cover completely with water.
2. Place the pot of water and egg over high heat.
3. Bring the egg to a boil.
4. Once boiling, set the timer for 9 minutes.
5. Transfer the egg from the boiling water to an ice bath.
6. Peel and enjoy.

SOFT/HARD-BOILED

For a perfectly soft-boiled egg:

1. Bring about 4 cups of water to a boil in a small pot. There should be enough water to cover the top of the egg.
2. Inspect your egg to make sure there are no cracks.
3. Place the egg in a slotted spoon and gently place it in the pot of boiling water.
4. Set your timer for 6 minutes.
5. Remove the egg from the pot and transfer it to an ice bath for 3 minutes.
6. Peel and enjoy.

> **Pro tip:** You can cook as many eggs as will fit comfortably at the bottom of your pot.

For a recipe using soft-boiled eggs, see page 53 (Soft-Boiled Egg and Avocado Toast).

SUNNY-SIDE UP

When it comes to sunny-side up eggs, steam is your best friend.

Here's the best way to make eggs sunny-side up:

1. Melt 1 tablespoon butter in a nonstick skillet over medium-low heat. Butter should be melted but not browning.
2. Crack the eggs directly into a (say it with me) *nonstick skillet.*

3. Sprinkle 2 tablespoons water on top of the eggs.
4. Cover and let cook over medium-low heat for 3 minutes, or until the whites have hardened and are firmly holding the yolk in place.
5. Serve with a little salt and pepper and enjoy.

> **Pro tip:** Please, please don't use a cast-iron pan or a skillet notorious for burning your food. My favorite nonstick skillet came from Walmart and set me back fifteen dollars. I use it every day and it has yet to disappoint.

FRIED

I used to love fried eggs. When I was in high school, I would make a fried egg sandwich almost every day. Here's how I did it:

1. Melt 1 tablespoon butter in a (I mean it!) nonstick skillet over medium heat.
2. Crack your egg into the skillet. Be careful not to break the yolk just yet.

3. After about a minute and a half, the whites of the egg should solidify. This is when you flip your egg.
4. For over easy, cook only for another 30 seconds, yolk side down.
5. For a soft yolk, cook for about 1 minute.
6. For a hard yolk, cook for 3 minutes.

> **Pro tip:** You can touch the top of the egg to see how done it is. If the egg feels squishy, your yolk is still runny. If there is little to no give, your yolk is completely cooked.

To experience a bit of my childhood, melt a piece of cheddar cheese on top and enjoy between two pieces of toast. Bon appétit!

MINI FRITTATAS

My husband, bless his soul, is far more of a people person than I am. I would never invite numerous people to my house for an impromptu brunch. I need a good week to five months to prepare myself for that much human interaction. So when he came to me and asked me to prepare brunch for his work buddies, let's just say I was slightly less than excited. Knowing I would need to reserve as much energy as possible to make it through the day, I came up with this quick and easy frittata recipe. It's perfect for those mornings when you just don't have the energy to deal with standing over a stove. Pop this dish in the oven for a few minutes while you take the extra time to get ready for the day. Easy peasy.

PREP TIME: 5 MINUTES ❤ **COOK TIME:** 35 MINUTES ❤ **SERVES:** 4–6

INGREDIENTS:

Oil or butter, for greasing
8 ounces Italian pork sausage
½ onion, sliced thin (about ½ cup)
1 green pepper, diced
1 cup spinach, packed
8 eggs
1 teaspoon Italian seasoning
¼ teaspoon salt
¼ teaspoon ground black pepper

Pro tip: This is a perfect recipe to make in bulk and save the leftovers in a container in the fridge.

DIRECTIONS:

1. Preheat the oven to 350°F. Grease the cups of a muffin pan.
2. Cook the sausage in a nonstick skillet over high heat. Slice using a spatula or rubber scraper. As the chunks of sausage sizzle and start to brown, crush with the head of your spatula or rubber scraper until the pieces of sausage are about ½–¼ inch thick.
3. Continue cooking and breaking up the sausage for 5 minutes, or until browned.
4. Add the onions and green pepper. Cook for another 5 minutes, stirring every minute. The onions and peppers should start to soften.
5. Mix in the spinach and cover for 2 minutes.
6. Divide the sausage mixture evenly in the prepared muffin pan.
7. Crack the eggs and add the seasonings into a medium bowl and whisk until completely combined, about 2 minutes.
8. Distribute the egg batter evenly in the muffin pan, filling to just below the top of each cup.
9. Bake in the oven and cook for 20 minutes. The frittatas should be fluffy, without any pools of liquid.

HAPPIER-THAN-EVER HASH

I love a good hash. It's pure, unedited, save the formalities, kind of amazing. Let's be honest: When you go out for breakfast, the eggs, potatoes, and bacon on the side usually end up in the same bite anyway. We might as well just put it all together, like all the time. That's the beauty of a hash: All your ingredients are enjoying each other's company from the beginning, just the way they want it. You only need one pot for this recipe. What's better than eating a delicious, low-cost meal and looking over to see only one dish to wash? Whoever said eating healthy was hard and expensive lied to us!

PREP TIME: 8 MINUTES ❤ **COOK TIME:** 20–25 MINUTES ❤ **SERVES:** 3–5

INGREDIENTS:

2 tablespoons butter

1 large potato, diced

1 large sweet potato, diced

1 red pepper, sliced

1 white onion, sliced

1 tablespoon olive oil

2 rosemary sprigs

1 cup spinach, packed

1 teaspoon garlic powder

1 teaspoon onion powder

1 teaspoon Italian seasoning

1 teaspoon crushed red pepper flakes

5 eggs

Pinch of salt

Pinch of ground black pepper

½ cup grated cheddar cheese

Pro tip: I burned the roof of my mouth because I couldn't wait to devour this meal. So, you know, be careful.

DIRECTIONS:

1. Melt the butter in a large skillet over high heat, for 1 minute.
2. Add the potato, sweet potato, red pepper, and onion to the skillet; drizzle with the oil.
3. Throw in the rosemary sprigs, cover, and cook for 3 minutes. Reduce the heat to medium and cook for 4 minutes.
4. Remove the lid. The potatoes should be soft and slightly browned on the bottom. The peppers should be soft and the onion translucent.
5. Stir to loosen any veggies from the bottom of the pan and add the spinach.
6. Cover again, this time cooking for 2 minutes. The spinach should be wilted and a darker shade of green.
7. Add the garlic powder, onion powder, Italian seasoning, and red pepper flakes, and mix until combined.
8. Crack the eggs in the center of the skillet on top of the veggie mixture, with each egg about an inch apart. Season with the salt and pepper.
9. Cover and cook over medium heat for 4 minutes. The egg whites should turn white while the yolks are still yellow, but not wet to the touch.
10. Sprinkle with the cheese, remove from the heat, and cover again. For runny yolk, let sit for 2 minutes. For soft yolk, let sit for 4 minutes. For hard yolk, let sit for 5 minutes.
11. Remove from the heat and serve.

SOFT-BOILED EGG AND AVOCADO TOAST

The first time I had avocado toast was at Navy Pier in downtown Chicago, hilariously enough. My husband and I took our second trip to date with just the two of us. We had very little time to ourselves and very little funds to do anything extravagant. The avocado toast at Navy Pier was just about as luxurious as we've ever been with food. The plate was gorgeous, and I was very pleased to discover that it tasted even better than it looked. The runny yolk added a nice velvety touch. At that moment I realized there was so much more to eggs than my childhood had shown me. I think I made my rendition of that dish for a week straight after that experience, partly to feel fancy, and partly because I couldn't get enough of it. Whether you can afford a trip to Navy Pier, a trip to Dubai, or just a trip to the living room, I believe everyone should be able to taste this luxurious dish.

PREP TIME: 10 MINUTES ❤ **COOK TIME:** 15 MINUTES ❤ **SERVES:** 2

INGREDIENTS:

1 avocado

¼ cup diced red onion

1 tablespoon olive oil

1 teaspoon salt

1 teaspoon ground black pepper

½ teaspoon red pepper flakes

4 slices bread, toasted

4 soft-boiled eggs (page 46), peeled and sliced

1. Make a vertical incision along the circumference of the avocado, splitting it into two halves. Remove the pit. Use a spoon to scoop the insides into a small bowl. Mash to desired thickness.
2. Add the onion, olive oil, salt, pepper, and red pepper flakes.
3. Mix until well combined.
4. Spread the avocado mixture on the bread.
5. Top with the egg slices.

Pro tip: For a picture-perfect dish, top with a few mixed microgreens, pickled red onions, and an extra drizzle of olive oil.

BANGIN' BREAKFAST BURRITO

I have very few guilty pleasures in life. One of them is the breakfast burrito found at your friendly neighborhood McDonald's. I created this recipe to feel less guilty about eating fast food, with the notion in mind that everything you make at home is good for you. That's how I let myself eat brownies most nights. I can feel the nutritionists coming for me now. Just let me live in peace! This burrito tastes heavenly, while preserving a sense of home-style cooking. I love it, and if you make it, I guarantee you'll love it too. For an extra kick, enjoy with hot sauce.

PREP TIME: 5 MINUTES ♥ **COOK TIME:** 25 MINUTES ♥ **SERVES:** 4

INGREDIENTS:

4 breakfast sausage patties

8-ounce can diced tomatoes and green chiles*

4 eggs

1 cup shredded Colby Jack cheese

2 tablespoons butter

4 large tortillas

* **Note:** I use RO-TEL brand canned tomatoes and green chiles.

DIRECTIONS:

1. Cook the sausage patties in a medium skillet over high heat. Two minutes after the meat starts to sizzle, flip it over. The patty should be browned on one side and raw on the other.
2. Turn the heat down to medium-low and let cook for 2 minutes.
3. Using the edge of your spatula, break the patties into small pieces.
4. Open the can of tomatoes and green chiles and drain in a strainer.
5. Pour the tomato and green chile mixture into the pan with the crumbled-up patties. The tomatoes and chiles should make a sizzling noise when they enter the pan.
6. Crack the eggs into a medium bowl and whisk vigorously, with either a fork or a whisk, until the eggs are completely combined, about 2 minutes.
7. Pour the eggs into the pan, scraping each side of the pan with a rubber scraper and folding the contents into the center of the pan until the eggs have formed. This should take 3–5 minutes.
8. Add the cheese and fold into the eggs until the cheese is completely melted, about 2 minutes.
9. Remove from the heat and set aside.
10. Melt ½ tablespoon of the butter in a large skillet or a griddle over high heat.
11. Place your tortilla in the skillet and add ½ cup of the egg mixture to the center of the tortilla.
12. Take the edge of the bottom of the tortilla and fold it upward, covering half of the egg mixture in the center. Fold the sides of the tortilla inward and the top edge of the tortilla down, covering the rest of the egg mixture.
13. Flip using a spatula and cook for 1 minute, sealing the edges of the tortilla.
14. Repeat steps 10–12 for the remaining tortillas.

> **Pro tip:** Meal-prep this recipe by cooking the egg filling ahead of time and storing in an airtight container in your fridge. Scoop ½ cup of the mixture into a tortilla in a hot pan and repeat the steps to fold.

B.E.L.T. (BACON, EGGS, LETTUCE, AND TOMATO) BENEDICT

The key to a good Benedict is the hollandaise sauce. That's the main focus of this recipe. Hollandaise is one of those sauces that seem difficult to make, but it's not hard at all once you get the hang of it. Hollandaise is what happens when discipline meets delicious. When you master it (and you will), the Best Brunch of the Year award is as good as yours. Congratulations! Smile for the camera. I love this dish. It tastes like something you'd find in a restaurant, but you get to enjoy it from the comfort of your home, and for a fraction of the cost.

PREP TIME: 5 MINUTES ❤ **COOK TIME:** 12 MINUTES ❤ **SERVES:** 4

INGREDIENTS:

HOLLANDAISE SAUCE

3 egg yolks

1 tablespoon fresh lemon juice

1 tablespoon Dijon mustard

1 stick (½ cup) butter or ghee

2 teaspoons lemon pepper seasoning

B.E.L.T.

8 bacon slices

2 English muffins

1 large tomato, cut into 8 thin slices

2 romaine lettuce leaves, cut in half

4 poached eggs (page 44)

Pro tip: The hollandaise requires separation of the egg whites from the yolks. To do this, crack one egg at a time and hold each half of the shell with the open end facing up. Slowly pour the yolk into the opposite shell and repeat, using the edge of the shell to cut off as much of the egg white as possible with each pass. Repeat this process until you're left with a yolk still intact. You can also separate the egg in your hands. Crack the egg into your hand close to the end of your palm and the beginning of your fingertips. Pass the egg in between your hands with your fingertips slightly open allowing the egg whites to seep through with each pass. Place the yolks in a separate bowl. (Obviously, if you use the hand method, wash your hands before continuing.) See page 44 for directions for the perfect poached egg.

FOR THE HOLLANDAISE SAUCE:

1. In a blender, combine the 3 egg yolks, lemon juice, and Dijon mustard. Blend for 10 seconds, or until smooth.
2. Heat the butter in a saucepan over high heat, stirring every few seconds, until the butter is bubbling but still a light shade of yellow.
3. Gradually (and carefully) pour the hot butter into the blender with the egg mixture on high speed, until it is combined and the sauce is a light yellow. It should be thick enough to coat the back of a spoon.
4. Add the lemon pepper seasoning and fold in with a spoon. Pour the sauce into a bowl and set aside.

FOR THE B.E.L.T.:

1. Cook the bacon in a skillet over medium-high heat for 2 minutes on each side.
2. Transfer to a plate lined with paper towels to absorb excess grease.
3. Toast the English muffins, either in the toaster or in a pan with a tablespoon of butter.
4. Cut each English muffin in half and fill each with two tomato slices, a piece of lettuce, a slice of bacon, and a poached egg, and pour the hollandaise sauce over it.
5. Serve warm.

CHAPTER FOUR

THE SWEET SIDE OF THE BREAD

This section is all about those not-so-savory breakfast moments. The cheat-day loves of your life. The "Yes, Sarah, I can throw a proper brunch" type of recipes. Baked goods are more than just cookies and pies, though we'll get to those little cuties later. Baked goods can be enjoyed before 5 p.m. and they should! I'll show you how.

B IS FOR BANANA BREAD

Wait! Don't throw away those too-ripe bananas! Let's use them to make banana bread. My kids genuinely love bananas, but they love their mama's banana bread even more. It is moist, it is freezer friendly, and after you bake it you can enjoy these little slices of heaven for days to come. It makes me so happy to put overlooked ingredients to good use in the kitchen. Taking us from black bananas to fluffy sweet bread is the perfect example of "waste not, want not." If, when life gives you lemons you make lemonade, then when life gives you bananas, you make banana bread. The best part is, you only need one bowl! (Fun fact: I sang the Gwen Stefani song every time I wrote out the word *bananas*.) If you're someone who does that too, let's eat this bread together and be besties forever!

PREP TIME: 10 MINUTES ❤ **COOK TIME:** 50 MINUTES ❤ **SERVES:** 8–10

INGREDIENTS:

4 overripe bananas (b-a-n-a-n-a-s!)

1 stick (½ cup) butter, melted

1 large egg

1 cup granulated sugar

1 teaspoon vanilla extract

1½ cups flour

2 teaspoons baking powder

½ teaspoon salt

½ teaspoon ground cardamom

1 cup glazed pecans (optional)

Pro tip: For an extra tasty treat, top bread slices with ice cream and caramel sauce.

DIRECTIONS:

1. Preheat the oven to 350°F. Grease a 9 x 5-inch loaf pan.
2. Mash the bananas until there are no large lumps.
3. Pour in the butter and mix well, working the bananas into a thick, soup-like consistency.
4. Add the egg and mix vigorously until well combined.*
5. Pour in the sugar and vanilla and mix until smooth.
6. In a separate bowl, combine the flour, baking powder, salt, and cardamom.
7. Dump the flour mixture into the banana mixture and combine until you have a fairly thick and sticky batter.
8. Fold in the pecans, if using, until they are evenly distributed.
9. Transfer to the prepared loaf pan.
10. Bake in the oven for 45 minutes, or until the top is a caramel-brown color and a toothpick, stuck in the center, comes out clean.
11. Slice and serve warm.

* **Note:** I like to use the KitchenAid for mixing, but a large bowl, a spoon, and a little elbow grease will still get this done in a pinch.

BEST BLUEBERRY MUFFINS

Do you know the muffin man who lives on Drury Lane? Okay, because he has been trying to get his hands on this muffin recipe for years! I had to create this recipe because my husband threatened to move us to Drury Lane for the proximity to lifelong muffins. That's marriage, though: give and take and muffin making. We adore blueberries, so I had to include them. These muffins are perfectly dense, delectably moist, and muffin-man-approved.

PREP TIME: 10 MINUTES ❤ **COOK TIME:** 25 MINUTES ❤ **YIELD:** 10 MUFFINS

INGREDIENTS:

1⅓ cups flour

¾ cup granulated sugar

2 teaspoons baking soda

½ teaspoon ground allspice

½ teaspoon salt

1 stick (½ cup) butter, melted

1 egg

2 teaspoons vanilla extract

⅓ cup milk

1 cup frozen blueberries

> **Pro tip:** Want even more out of these muffins? Try adding ½ cup frozen cranberries along with the blueberries.

DIRECTIONS:

1. Preheat the oven to 350°F. Line 10 cups of a muffin pan.
2. In a medium bowl, combine the flour, sugar, baking soda, allspice, and salt.
3. Mix until well combined. Set aside.
4. In a separate bowl, beat together the butter, egg, and vanilla until fully combined.
5. Add the milk to the egg mixture and stir for about 30 seconds, until thoroughly combined.
6. Gradually add the flour mixture to the egg mixture until they are fully incorporated and becomes a thick and sticky dough.
7. Fold in the blueberries with a spoon.
8. Spoon the batter into the muffin liners, only about ¾ full. Overfilling the cups will cause the batter to spill over.
9. Bake for 20–25 minutes, until a toothpick comes out clean.
10. Serve warm on any day that needs a little extra yum.

COFFEE CAKE

Okay, don't laugh at me, but my first experience with coffee cakes was those Little Debbie brand treats that come in a plastic bag. I was five or six years old, and my mom bought a box of these miraculous little cakes to pack as a treat in my lunches. My lunchtime possibilities changed forever after that day. I was bullied a lot as a kid. I've been as tall as a giraffe my whole life and have worn a size-ten shoe since the fourth grade. On those particularly rough days, this little cake meant the world to me. I had to capture that essence in a recipe. Yes, I have had other coffee cakes since those awkward school days. No, none of them have made my heart leap for joy like the first time. I'm sharing this recipe with you so our hearts may leap together.

PREP TIME: 30 MINUTES ❤ **COOK TIME:** 1 HOUR ❤ **SERVES:** 8–10

INGREDIENTS:

CAKE:

2 cups flour

2 teaspoons baking powder

2 teaspoons ground allspice

1 teaspoon salt

1 stick (½ cup) butter, softened*

½ cup granulated sugar

⅓ cup brown sugar

1 egg

¾ cup milk

2 teaspoons vanilla extract

FILLING:

2 tablespoons butter

2 teaspoons ground cinnamon

3 tablespoons brown sugar

3 apples, peeled, cored, and sliced thin

TOPPING:

½ cup flour

½ teaspoon ground cinnamon

½ teaspoon ground allspice

½ cup brown sugar

4 tablespoons (¼ cup) butter, at room temperature*

* **Note:** Make sure the butter is *not* melted. Your butter needs to be just soft enough to work with.

DIRECTIONS:

FOR THE CAKE:

1. Combine the flour, baking powder, allspice, and salt in a bowl and set aside.
2. Beat the butter, granulated sugar, and brown sugar until well combined.
3. Add the egg and beat until incorporated, about 1 minute.
4. Pour in the milk and vanilla and mix. The batter should look fairly pale and watery.
5. Slowly stir in the flour mixture until everything is combined, creating a thicker batter.

FOR THE FILLING:

1. Combine the butter, cinnamon, and brown sugar in a small saucepan over medium-high heat.
2. Add the apples and cook, covered, over low heat for about 10 minutes, until fork-tender.

FOR THE TOPPING:

1. Combine the flour, cinnamon, allspice, and brown sugar in a small bowl.
2. Mix the butter into the flour mixture with a fork, or your fingers, until small crumbs form.

Recipe Continues

PUT IT ALL TOGETHER:

1. Preheat the oven to 350°F. Grease a 9 x 9-inch baking pan.
2. Pour half of the batter into the pan.
3. Smooth the batter with a rubber spatula until there is an even layer on the bottom of the pan.
4. Spoon in the apple filling along with its leftover juices from the saucepan, spreading evenly on top of the batter.
5. Cover the apples with the remaining batter and smooth into a second even layer.
6. Sprinkle with the topping and bake in the oven for 45–50 minutes, until a toothpick inserted in the center comes out clean and the top is golden brown.
7. Let sit for 10 minutes to cool before serving.

Pro tip: It's in the name. Seriously, don't skip enjoying this with a cup of coffee.

DELIGHTFUL DONUTS

There's a donut shop within walking distance of my house, and they make the best donuts I've ever tasted. No, I'm not telling you whether or not I walk there every day. Mind your business! The craziest part is that the dough at this donut shop is the same for every flavor. The glory comes from the toppings. Inspired by these simple, glorious donuts, I created a couple of easy, fun, and downright delightful donut recipes of my own. These beauties come in two varieties: simple sugar donuts and a cereal donut. The second one is for those of us who loved eating cereal and watching cartoons as kids (and probably still do if you're a parent). Pick your style, make them both, or create your own. That's what cooking is about, having fun and discovering something deliciously new. Enjoy with fresh strawberries and blueberries.

SIMPLE SUGAR DONUTS

PREP TIME: 5 MINUTES ❤ **COOK TIME:** 20 MINUTES ❤ **SERVES:** 4

INGREDIENTS:

1 cup granulated sugar

1 tablespoon ground cinnamon

3 cups canola oil

16-ounce can jumbo biscuits (8 count)

DIRECTIONS:

1. Combine the sugar and cinnamon in a medium bowl. Set aside.
2. Pour the oil into a 3-quart saucepan.
3. Heat the oil over medium-high heat for about 5 minutes. (To test if oil is ready, add a drop of water to the pan. If it crackles, it's ready.)
4. While you are waiting for the oil to heat up, open and separate the biscuits on a clean workspace.
5. Cut a donut hole in the center of each biscuit by pressing down with the edge of a spoon* and wiggling it back and forth until the biscuit dough separates. Repeat this process until you have a circular hole in the center. The hole can range in size from 1 to 2 inches. Remove the center and set aside. (You'll be frying this part too to make donut holes!)

6. Carefully place the biscuits and donut holes, two sets of two at a time, into the oil with a slotted spoon. The dough will nearly double in size and become a golden-brown color. This should take 1–2 minutes.
7. Flip the donut and repeat for the other side.
8. Remove from the oil and hold them over the pan for a few seconds to shake off any excess oil.
9. Place the donuts in the cinnamon sugar and, with a sifting motion, shake the bowl to coat them in sugar.
10. Transfer to a plate lined with paper towels.

* **Note:** You can use a small container like an empty pill bottle to create donut holes instead of a spoon. Place the bottle open-side down onto the biscuit. Push hard and wiggle the bottle to separate the two pieces of dough.

Simple Sugar Donuts, page 67

CINNAMON TOAST CRUNCH DONUT

INGREDIENTS:

1 cup granulated sugar

1 tablespoon ground cinnamon

1 cup Cinnamon Toast Crunch cereal*

1 cup powdered sugar

$\frac{1}{4}$ cup plus 1 tablespoon heavy cream

3 cups canola oil

16-ounce can jumbo biscuits (8 count)

* **Note:** I'm using Cinnamon Toast Crunch cereal, but you can use anything you want, from Honey Nut Cheerios, to Froot Loops, to Oreos. Really, whatever makes your mouth water.

> **Pro tip:** Test-fry one donut hole before frying the whole batch. If the donut browns too quickly (within 5–10 seconds), the oil is too hot. It's better to mess up one small donut hole than ruin a whole batch of donuts.

DIRECTIONS:

1. Combine the sugar and cinnamon in a medium bowl. Set aside.
2. Crumble the cereal in a zip-top bag on the counter by smashing with your hand for about 1 minute. There should be a mixture of both larger and smaller pieces of crushed cereal bits.
3. Pour the sugar into a bowl and add the cream. Stir until fully combined. The icing mixture should be runny with no clumps.
4. Pour the oil into a 3-quart saucepan.
5. Heat the oil over medium-high heat for about 5 minutes. (To test if the oil is ready, add a drop of water to the pan. If it starts to crackle, it's ready.)
6. While you are waiting for the oil to heat up, open and separate the biscuits on a clean workspace.
7. Cut a donut hole in the center of each biscuit by pressing down with the edge of a spoon* and wiggling it back and forth until the biscuit dough separates. Repeat this process until you have a circular hole in the center of the biscuit. The hole can range in size from 1 to 2 inches. Remove the center and set aside. (You'll be frying this part too to make donut holes!)
8. Carefully place the biscuits and donut holes, two sets of two at a time, into the oil with a slotted spoon. The dough will nearly double in size and become a golden-brown color. This should take 1–2 minutes.
9. Flip the donuts and repeat for the other side.
10. Remove from the oil and hold them over the pan for a few seconds to shake off any excess oil.
11. Place the donuts in the sugar cinnamon and, with a sifting motion, shake the bowl to coat them in sugar.
12. Transfer to a cooling rack laid over parchment paper. This will stop the icing from forming undesirable puddles and make cleaning up a breeze.
13. Using a spoon, drizzle the icing over the donuts and top with the crushed cereal.

* **Note:** You can use a small container like an empty pill bottle to create donut holes instead of a spoon. Place the bottle open-side down onto the biscuit. Push hard and wiggle the bottle to separate the two pieces of dough.

LUKE'S MONKEY BREAD

My son is an avid fan of my monkey bread. There's nothing better than seeing his tiny face light up when I bring this gorgeous, dome-shaped, caramelized bread to the table. Now he asks if he can help me make it. I always say yes. I need to pass the torch to someone. If this recipe can get all of my kids in the kitchen cooking, I know it can do the same for you. Bring out this recipe for your next brunch, sit back, and soak in the smiles of your guests. You did that, you rock star! My son is allergic to nuts so we don't add them, but you can easily throw in a few pecans, walnuts, or any other nut of your liking for a little extra crunch.

PREP TIME: 10 MINUTES ♥ **COOK TIME:** 25 MINUTES ♥ **SERVES:** 4–6

INGREDIENTS:

2 cups granulated sugar

2½ teaspoons ground cinnamon

Two 16-ounce cans jumbo biscuits (8 count each)

1 stick (½ cup) butter

½ cup brown sugar

1 teaspoon vanilla extract

Budget tip: This recipe can double as a dessert and is a great cost-effective option for hosting an intimate party for all ages.

DIRECTIONS:

1. Preheat the oven to 350°F. Grease a Bundt pan.

2. In a large bowl, combine the granulated sugar and cinnamon, and set aside.

3. Remove the biscuits from the packaging and cut each biscuit into fourths. Toss the biscuit pieces in the cinnamon sugar, working in batches to avoid crowding the bowl.

4. Transfer to the prepared Bundt pan.

5. Melt the butter in a small saucepan over low heat.

6. Add the brown sugar, vanilla, and cinnamon sugar. Mix until almost completely combined. You should be able to see small pockets of melted butter in the pan.

7. Pour in a circular motion over the biscuits in the Bundt pan, coating them evenly.

8. Bake in the oven for 25 minutes, or until the biscuits have almost doubled in size and are browned on top. To check for doneness, use a knife to separate some of the biscuits. If they look doughy, leave them in for another 2–3 minutes, until baked through.

9. Let the bread cool for 5 minutes.

10. Dump upside-down on a plate and serve.

Mmm, Sorry I'm on My Lunch

It's lunchtime, you made it! Whether you work for a company, for yourself, for that degree, or for your family, lunchtime, in my opinion, is a symbol of success. Why, just today my daughter had a tantrum for five minutes because she thought she lost her doll's comb (it was behind her), my other daughter is at the stage where a forceful *no* is her favorite word, and my son was demanding my attention as I scrambled between one disaster and the other. Before noon today, I soothed a meltdown, scrubbed crayon off the wall (again), did laundry, washed dishes, wrote some of this lovely book, had story time, played outside, fed the tiny humans twice, and put said humans down for a much-needed nap. Success! Time to celebrate by feeding my body an energy-packed lunch to keep me going so I can tackle the second half of my day. It's not just lunchtime, it's *me* time. These recipes feed my soul and encourage me to keep living life to the fullest. My wish is that they do the same for you. I've broken these recipes into three chapters: soups, sandwiches, and salads. For lunchtime, can we all just yell (or whisper—it's nap time over here), "Success!"?

CHAPTER FIVE

SOUP(ISH)

I confess I'm in a low-maintenance relationship with soup. It's not too demanding because it understands that I'm busy. I had no idea how strongly I felt about soup until I got married, had kids, and needed to feed my clan. It's a low-effort, long-lasting meal that feels like a warm hug for our bellies. I want to personally thank the genius who originally decided to throw a bunch of stuff in some broth and serve it. I know for sure parents everywhere cheered, "Yes! Now there's a cause I can get behind. Soup genius, we salute you." Soup is so easy and yummy, you might be thinking, "How can it get any better?" Well, let me show you. If you want low-cost cooking, soup is your friend. You can make a lot for very little, and sneak in veggies without a peep from picky toddlers. In this chapter you'll find recipes for my absolute favorite soups. Some are dear to me for nostalgic reasons, and some for how quickly they come together. But I love all of them because they're easy on the wallet and packed full of flavor.

CHEDDAR BROCCOLI SOUP

I know I am not the inventor of broccoli soup. Many establishments and households have taken a whack at this binge-worthy soup. My affair with broccoli cheddar soup started with the pregnancy of my third daughter. I haven't met one pregnant lady who went without a craving her whole pregnancy. It's a rite of passage. Make a baby, indulge in a craving or two. With my third, my craving was soup. While this craving was healthier than the one I had with my first born (double cheeseburgers at midnight), ordering it from restaurants was a little too pricey for me. So I came up with this recipe. It's easy to whip up a batch, store it in the fridge, and snack on it all week. Enjoy this with your favorite bread for dipping.

PREP TIME: 5 MINUTES ❤ **COOK TIME:** 40 MINUTES ❤ **SERVES:** 6-8

INGREDIENTS:

2 tablespoons butter

1 teaspoon minced garlic

1 small red onion, thinly sliced

1 small yellow onion, thinly sliced

2 cups (16 ounces) frozen broccoli

1 cup matchstick carrots

3 cups chicken broth

2 cups heavy cream

2 teaspoons salt

2 teaspoons garlic powder

2 teaspoons onion powder

1 tablespoon lemon pepper seasoning

2 cups shredded mild cheddar cheese

2 cups shredded Colby Jack cheese

DIRECTIONS:

1. Melt the butter in a large pot over medium heat and swirl it so it covers the bottom of the pot. This should take about 30 seconds.

2. Add the garlic and onions, reduce the heat to low, and cook until the garlic is fragrant and the onions are translucent, about 10 minutes.

3. Add the broccoli and cover. Cook for an additional 15 minutes, or until the broccoli is defrosted and soft, stirring every 3 to 5 minutes.

4. Add the carrots and broth. Bring to a simmer and cook for an additional 15 minutes, or until the carrots are limp and the broccoli is a deeper shade of green.

5. Pour in the cream, salt, garlic powder, onion powder, lemon pepper seasoning, and both cheeses, until the cheese is thoroughly combined and the soup has turned a soft yellow color.

6. Serve warm.

Pro tip: Visit www.ChefLexyRogers.com to see how to make the best bread bowl. Then put this soup inside it!

ANYTHING-BUT-BASIC TOMATO SOUP

I heard of tomato soup in a movie once when I was a kid. Yeah, this woman was bathing in the stuff after being sprayed by a skunk. After watching that, I never thought I would eat it. Years later, when I started getting serious about expanding my palate, I tried some tomato soup. It was, for lack of a better word, disgusting. The overpowering acidity combined with underwhelming seasoning left a horrid taste in my mouth. But that did not stop me from trying again, and again, and again, until finally I decided to make it for myself. I don't know why I was so determined to like the stuff after so many failed attempts. I made the soup and I made it good! My husband and I ate it for a week straight afterward. If you do that too, we promise not to judge. Remember to serve this with grilled cheese sandwiches; it's the law.

PREP TIME: 10 MINUTES ♥ **COOK TIME:** 20 MINUTES ♥ **SERVES:** 10

INGREDIENTS:

1 tablespoon olive oil

1 tablespoon minced garlic

2 red bell peppers, sliced

1 yellow bell pepper, sliced

1 orange bell pepper, sliced

1 medium white onion, chopped

2 medium red onions, roughly chopped

30 ounces (about 5 cups) grape tomatoes

2 cups water

1 rosemary sprig

1 chicken bouillon cube

1 cup fresh basil leaves, plus more for garnish (optional)

2 tablespoons granulated sugar

1 tablespoon Creole seasoning*

1 teaspoon chopped chives, plus more for garnish (optional)

¼ cup heavy cream (optional)

* **Note:** I like to use Tony Chachere's Creole Seasoning.

> **Pro tip:** This soup does well in the fridge for about two weeks and in the freezer for a few months.

DIRECTIONS:

1. Drizzle the oil into a large pot over medium-high heat.
2. Add the garlic, peppers, and onions and cook for about 5 minutes. Stir occasionally to keep the garlic from burning.
3. Add the tomatoes, water, rosemary, and bouillon cube.*
4. Cover and cook for 10 minutes, or until the tomatoes have broken down and the peppers and onions are soft. The soup should be fragrant and slightly bubbling.
5. Transfer to a blender and blend until smooth. You can also use an immersion blender. (Be careful! Hot soup can splash.)
6. Add the basil, sugar, Creole seasoning, and chives to the blender. Blend on high for 30 seconds.
7. Slowly add the cream, if using, while blending, and then blend for another 30 seconds. (The cream is optional here; the soup is just as lovely without it.)
8. Pour into bowls, garnish with extra basil, chives, and cream if desired, and serve.

* **Note:** I like to press down on the tomatoes with a slotted spoon to pop them open and speed up the cooking process when I'm in a pinch.

NOT YA MAMA'S CHILI

Chili is a budget builder's dream. When I'm in a tight financial spot, chili is one of my go-to meals. We can make a large pot for less than 10 dollars and have enough leftovers to feed the entire family for days. The best part about chili is that it tastes better day after day. The longer chili sits, the bolder the flavor grows. If you have the time to simmer it all day, you'll get a depth of flavor that can't be achieved through the minimum amount of cooking time. Feel free to customize this chili however you like. Throw in a variety of toppings to make this fabulous dish even better. No matter how you make this recipe, you won't be able to eat it without a smile.

PREP TIME: 12 MINUTES ❤ **COOK TIME:** 1–2 HOURS ❤ **SERVES:** 8–10

INGREDIENTS:

1½ pounds sausage or ground beef

Two 15.5-ounce cans black beans, drained and rinsed

Two 15.5-ounce cans dark red kidney beans, drained and rinsed

Two 15.5-ounce cans pinto beans, drained and rinsed

14.5-ounce can fire-roasted tomatoes

Two 15-ounce cans tomato sauce

2 cups water

1 medium red onion, thinly sliced

1 medium white onion, thinly sliced

¼ cup chili powder

2 tablespoons garlic powder

2 tablespoons onion powder

1 teaspoon cayenne pepper

2 fresh oregano sprigs

DIRECTIONS:

1. Brown and crumble the meat in a large nonstick stock pot over high heat for 5 minutes.*
2. Reduce the heat, add the beans, tomatoes, tomato sauce, water, and onions and stir until combined.
3. Add the chili powder, garlic powder, onion powder, and cayenne pepper and stir thoroughly.
4. Throw in the oregano sprigs and reduce the heat to low.
5. Cover and cook for a minimum of 1 hour if using pork or turkey sausage, and a minimum of 2 hours for beef. (You can leave this to simmer on the lowest heat setting for as long as you like. The longer it simmers, the more complex the flavor.)

* **Note:** If you opted for ground beef with a fat content higher than 7 percent, drain the grease from the pot after browning.

Budget tip: The meat is the most expensive ingredient in this recipe. If funds are tight, you can still enjoy this soup without meat.

THE LOUISE DIP SOUP

The inspiration for this recipe came from someone very special to me. My Aunt Louise was one of the most amazing individuals you could ever hope to meet. She was gorgeous, smart, and witty. Our families would get together at least once a week when I was growing up. I'll always remember those good conversations over a plate of yummy food. Unfortunately my aunt isn't here anymore, but memories of her are. The fastest way to bring back her memory is by enjoying a dip she used to make. To this day, nostalgia aside, Aunt Louise's dip is my favorite dip of all time. I did, however, start feeling a little bad about eating chips and dip almost every day. So I turned her velvety dip into a stunning soup. With no more than five key ingredients and fifteen minutes you can share a literal piece of heaven with me. This is best served with bread.

PREP TIME: 2 MINUTES ♥ **COOK TIME:** 20 MINUTES ♥ **SERVES:** 4–6

INGREDIENTS:

1 pound Italian sausage

10-ounce can diced tomatoes and green chilies*

8-ounce package cream cheese (about 1 cup)

2 cups heavy cream

2 cups chicken broth (see Budget tip)

3 tablespoons Creole seasoning**

Fresh green onions, chopped

* **Note:** I use RO-TEL brand canned tomatoes and green chiles.

** **Note:** I like to use Tony Chachere's Creole Seasoning.

DIRECTIONS:

1. In a pot over high heat, brown and crumble the sausage. This should take 5 minutes.
2. Add the tomatoes and green chiles and stir to combine.
3. Add the cream cheese and stir until melted and fully combined, about 3 minutes.
4. Pour in the cream and chicken broth. Let simmer for 10 minutes.
5. Add the Creole seasoning and stir thoroughly.
6. Garnish with the green onions and serve.

Budget tip: The more broth you add, the thinner the texture will be and the more bowls you can serve.

Pro tip: Removing the heavy cream and broth will leave you with a dip perfect for every chip and veggie you can think of.

GIMME DAT GUMBO

Gumbo is not a dish I grew up eating, but it makes my pocketbook happy. I love flexible meals that can be altered but still retain their flavor. My grandma Mama Anne could walk into the kitchen and fix something amazing with simple ingredients. This soup reminds me of her. I like to imagine somewhere, in the heart of Louisiana, a grandma much like mine is grinning, knowing she can transform scraps into a wholesome meal. You can have this soup with or without the meat, or with extra seafood or none at all. You can add or take away veggies, and you can swap seasonings for your own personal favorites. The only thing you *cannot* do is forget the roux. This dish is all about the roux. The full-bodied, subtle, peanut-flavored sauce is what makes this gumbo sing. Hey, if my hubby can make it perfectly (with a little instruction), I know you can too. This gumbo is great with rice.

PREP TIME: 10 MINUTES ❤ **COOK TIME:** 1 HOUR ❤ **SERVES:** 10–12

INGREDIENTS:

ROUX:

1 stick (½ cup) butter

½ cup flour

2 tablespoons Creole seasoning*

GUMBO:

13.5-ounce package andouille sausage

2 medium white onions, sliced

7 celery ribs, chopped

2 green peppers, sliced

7 cups water

1 beef bouillon cube

1 chicken bouillon cube

2 bay leaves

1 tablespoon butter

1 pound chicken breast

1 pound frozen raw shrimp, thawed, deveined, and tails removed

* **Note:** I like to use Tony Chachere's Creole Seasoning.

DIRECTIONS:

FOR THE ROUX:

1. Melt the butter in a pot over medium heat.
2. Once the butter starts to bubble, add the flour and Creole seasoning. Mix until a thick paste forms.
3. Reduce the heat to medium-low.
4. Stir about every 5 minutes for the next hour. (I like to complete one soup-related task and then check on my roux to stir it and adjust the heat if needed.)*
5. The roux is finished when it is a nice chocolate-brown color. The roux will also be thin and runny.
6. Remove from the heat and stir until the roux has cooled before adding it to the soup.

*Note: The roux will go through four major stages. In the first stage, it will be pale and thick with no distinctive smell. As the flour continues to cook, the roux will get progressively darker, and the smell will gradually get nuttier and more full-bodied. For more on the perfect roux, see pages 13–14.

FOR THE GUMBO:

1. Cut the sausage into two halves lengthwise. Then cut each half into 1-inch slices.

Recipe Continues

2. Cook the sausage in a large pot over medium-high heat until browned, about 10 minutes.

3. Add the onion, celery, peppers, water, beef and chicken bouillon cubes, and bay leaves. Cook until the veggies are soft, about 20 minutes.

4. Melt the butter in a skillet over high heat and sear the chicken on each side for 2 minutes. Transfer to a cutting board and cut chicken into cubes. The chicken will finish cooking in the soup.

5. Add the chicken to the soup, reduce the heat, and simmer about 5 minutes.

6. Add the cooled roux, stirring to combine.

7. While the soup is simmering, add the shrimp and cook for 10 minutes before serving.

Budget tip: The meat is the most expensive ingredient in this recipe. If funds are tight, you can still enjoy this soup without meat. Add a can of black beans and a can of red kidney beans instead of meat for a cheaper option.

CHAPTER SIX

WHY YES, I'D LOVE A SANDWICH

The sandwich: It's a classic staple of lunchtime foods, and one of my personal go-tos. I am not, however, going to give you a recipe for ham and cheese or peanut butter and jelly. Oh no, these recipes are full of flavor and flare. Some might say they push the boundaries of what can truly be classified as a sandwich. To that I say, rules are meant to be broken. When you taste these sandwiches, I have a feeling you'll agree with me.

NOT-FROM-PHILLY CHEESESTEAK

I want to start by saying I have never been to Philadelphia for an original Philly cheesesteak. Despite that embarrassing fact, this is my favorite sandwich in the whole world (granted, I've only been to maybe max ten of the fifty states . . . so far). Does not matter; I will probably brag about this sandwich until the day I die. I like to think of myself as an active cheesesteak advocate. I have tried many a cheesesteak from many an establishment. None, might I note, has the compound awesomeness of the recipe that I am sharing with you here. She is my favorite child (don't tell my other children!). Treat her with care.

PREP TIME: 15 MINUTES ♥ **COOK TIME:** 20 MINUTES ♥ **SERVES:** 4–6

INGREDIENTS:

1 tablespoon avocado oil (or olive oil)

2 green peppers, sliced

1 medium white onion, sliced

8 ounces baby bella mushrooms, sliced

2 teaspoons lemon pepper seasoning

1 pound shaved steak (ribeye or your preference)

2 tablespoons butter

⅓ cup mayonnaise

1 tablespoon Creole seasoning*

12-ounce loaf French bread

4 slices pepper Jack cheese

4 slices provolone cheese

* **Note:** I like to use Tony Chachere's Creole Seasoning.

> **Budget tip:** A foot-long sandwich feeds my whole family of five. If you don't need as much food, go slider style! Make single servings by using a ciabatta bun, Hawaiian roll, or regular sliced bread. Save the rest of the filling in the fridge and make sandwiches throughout the week.

DIRECTIONS:

1. Preheat the oven to 375°F.
2. Heat the oil in a pan over medium-low heat. Add the peppers, onions, mushrooms, and season with lemon pepper seasoning.
3. Cook for about 7 minutes, until the onions are translucent and the mushrooms have released liquids into the pan. The peppers should be cooked al dente, just enough so their color has lightened, and they do not taste raw but are still somewhat firm.
4. Remove from the heat and set aside.
5. Melt the butter in a cast-iron pan or nonstick skillet over high heat and cook the steak for 5–8 minutes until cooked through.
6. Mix the mayonnaise with the Creole seasoning and set aside.
7. Cut the bread loaf lengthwise without cutting it completely in half. Spread the seasoned mayo on both halves of the inside of the bread.
8. Top with the steak, veggies, and cheeses, alternating between a slice of pepper Jack and a slice of provolone.
9. Transfer to a baking sheet. Bake in the oven for 5 minutes, or until the cheese is melted and the bread is toasted.

> **Pro tip:** Maximize your leftovers by switching things up. Use the filling on top of fries, or stuff it inside lettuce leaves for a low-carb option.

JOEY'S MEATBALL SUB

Any *Friends* fans in the house? One of my favorite episodes is the one where Joey, while on a ride along with a cop in New York City, throws himself across Ross in the backseat after hearing a gunshot. The sound was actually a car backfiring. But the funny part is, instead of risking his life to save his friend Ross, he risked his life to grab his meatball sub. I don't know exactly how that sandwich tasted, but I bet it was pretty darn good. This recipe is my interpretation of that sandwich. Enjoy this sandwich made of gooey mozzarella, crispy buttered bread, tender meatballs, and bold marinara. An invention so perfect you might rescue it from a backfiring car yourself.

PREP TIME: 15 MINUTES ❤ **COOK TIME:** 30 MINUTES ❤ **YIELD:** 8–10 SANDWICHES

INGREDIENTS:

8 ounces Italian sausage

8 ounces lean ground beef

2 eggs

2 teaspoons dried parsley

1 teaspoon garlic powder

1 teaspoon onion powder

1 teaspoon Italian seasoning

½ teaspoon salt

½ teaspoon ground black pepper

¼ cup heavy cream

½ cup Italian bread crumbs

½ cup grated Parmesan or Romano cheese

24-ounce jar marinara sauce

10 hoagie rolls

Butter for the rolls

Sliced provolone cheese (optional)

> **Budget tip:** Save leftover meatballs and marinara and make spaghetti for dinner! Check out page 160 for tips on making fresh pasta.

DIRECTIONS:

1. Preheat the oven to 350°F. Line a 9 x 13-inch baking dish with foil.

2. In a large bowl, mix the sausage and ground beef until evenly combined.

3. Crack the eggs into a separate bowl and mix in the parsley, garlic powder, onion powder, Italian seasoning, salt, and pepper until the whites of the eggs are no longer visible.

4. Pour the eggs into the meat and combine with gloved hands.

5. Add the cream, bread crumbs, and Parmesan or Romano cheese, mixing to combine.

6. Use a tablespoon to create forty rounded meatballs and place them in the prepared baking dish. Space the meatballs about 1 inch apart. Use two separate dishes if necessary.

7. Bake in the oven for 20–25 minutes, until the meatballs are cooked through and browned on the tops.

8. Pour the marinara sauce into a saucepan and heat over medium-low heat.

9. Transfer the meatballs to the saucepan and toss them in the marinara sauce to coat. Remove from the heat.

10. Heat a skillet over medium-high heat. Cut the rolls lengthwise without cutting completely in half. Butter each half of the inside of the bread. Toast for 2 minutes in the skillet, then plate and immediately top with the provolone, if using, to melt.

11. Spoon about four meatballs into each sandwich. Cover with extra marinara and serve.

PICKLE MY FRIED CHICKEN SANDWICH

Anyone remember when Popeyes came out with the fried chicken sandwich that was coveted almost as much as a new pair of Jordans on release day? I was living in Kenosha, Wisconsin, at the time, about a five-minute drive from one of the establishments. It took me almost four months to get my hands on one of those bad boys. Lines of cars stopped up the street, honking at non-chicken purchasers just trying to make it home from work. When I did actually try it for the first time, my immediate thought was, "Mmm, I can make it better." Fun fact: Most times when I go to a restaurant, I try to gauge how well I can re-create the dish I ordered. I think I did this particular dish justice, but you can be the judge of that.

PREP TIME: 1 HOUR AND 5 MINUTES ❤ **COOK TIME:** 12 MINUTES ❤ **YIELD:** 8 SANDWICHES

INGREDIENTS:

4 chicken breasts (about 2 pounds)

1½ cups pickle juice

2 cups flour

1 tablespoon cornstarch

1 tablespoon Creole seasoning*

1 teaspoon paprika

2 eggs

2 cups canola oil

8 sandwich buns

Pickle spears

Mayonnaise (for spreading)

* **Note:** I like to use Tony Chachere's Creole Seasoning.

DIRECTIONS:

1. Cut each chicken breast in half horizontally. Transfer to a bowl and pour pickle juice over it.
2. Cover and refrigerate for a minimum of 1 hour.
3. In a separate bowl, mix the flour, cornstarch, Creole seasoning, and paprika. The flour should look visibly seasoned. If it doesn't, season it more.
4. Beat the eggs in a separate bowl to create the egg wash.
5. Remove the chicken from the pickle juice, coat in the flour, and dip into the egg wash. Dredge once more in the flour and dust off any excess by gently shaking the chicken.
6. Heat the oil in a deep skillet over high heat.
7. Cook the chicken in the oil for 6 minutes on each side.
8. Transfer to a plate lined with a paper towel to drain excess oil.
9. Place each piece of chicken on a bottom sandwich bun and top with the pickles and mayonnaise before placing the top bun. Serve warm.

TACO: THE SANDWICH'S COUSIN

Is a taco a sandwich? Technically, no. Will that stop me from listing this irresistible deliciousness of a recipe in the sandwich chapter? Also no. If you find a good taco joint, you're not going to cheat on said joint with a different one just to test it out. Good tacos don't grow on trees. I'm here to say, next to nothing is worse than craving a taco and getting served a bland mess in a Styrofoam box. The good news is, I have created an amazing taco recipe for you. So go ahead and cross "turn my kitchen into my favorite taco joint" off your bucket list.

PREP TIME: 5 MINUTES ❤ **COOK TIME:** 8 MINUTES ❤ **SERVES:** 3–4

INGREDIENTS:

1 pound raw shrimp, deveined, tails removed, and rinsed

1 tablespoon olive oil

1½ teaspoons Sazón seasoning*

¼ teaspoon red pepper flakes*

1 mango, peeled and cubed**

1 red onion, diced

5 ounces diced tomatoes

1 tablespoon fresh chopped cilantro

1 teaspoon fresh-squeezed lime juice

1 teaspoon salt

1 teaspoon pepper

6–8 tortillas

Lime wedges (for serving, optional)

* **Note:** You can omit the red pepper flakes if hot and spicy isn't your jam, and you can swap out the Sazón for your favorite all-in-one seasoning.

** **Note:** If you've never worked with mango before, the pit runs through the entire middle of the fruit. Cut on each side of the pit so that you have two end pieces of flesh and one flesh-covered pit. On both end pieces, score the inside, making equal vertical and horizontal lines, creating rows of tiny squares. Avoid cutting the skin. Gently separate the flesh cubes from the skin with your knife.

DIRECTIONS:

1. Place the shrimp in a bowl and add the oil, Sazón, and red pepper flakes. Stir until they are thoroughly coated.

2. Cook the shrimp in an air fryer on 360°F for 6 minutes, or until they have turned pink and are white and juicy on the inside. You can also fry these in a pan on the stovetop over low heat for the same amount of time.

3. In a separate bowl, combine the mango, onion, tomatoes, cilantro, lime juice, salt, and pepper.

4. Heat the tortillas in a dab of butter or oil in a pan over medium-low heat.

5. Place the shrimp and mango salsa on the tortillas and serve with the lime wedges, if using.

Pro tip: For a tempura-style crunchy shrimp, beat 1 egg with 1 cup sifted flour, 2 tablespoons cornstarch, and ½ cup water in a stand mixer until pale yellow and fluffy. Dip the shrimp in the batter and fry in 3 cups canola oil for 2–3 minutes.

BETTER-THAN-BEST BURGER

Burgers are a creative food lover's best friend. They are insanely delicious, and the combo possibilities are endless. (I could write an entire separate book based solely on different burger combos.) If you want a blank-slate meal, grab a burger. The hardest part about making a burger is perfecting the patty. Once you do that, the rest is just a big ol' love affair between that burger and your stomach. This recipe is my favorite way to eat a burger, but of course you can top it however you like. Want a low-carb option? Ditch the buns for two leaves of lettuce (my personal preference). Just don't tweak the patty, okay? I've made a lot of burgers and this patty comes out juicy and packed with flavor every single time. Since people easily charge ten to fifteen dollars for dry, crumbly burgers, you'll definitely get your money's worth with this burger.

PREP TIME: 10 MINUTES ❤ **COOK TIME:** 10 MINUTES ❤ **YIELD:** 12 PATTIES

INGREDIENTS:

2 pounds lean ground beef

1 egg

¼ cup heavy cream

½ cup bread crumbs

1 teaspoon garlic powder

1 teaspoon onion powder

1 teaspoon lemon pepper seasoning

1 teaspoon soy sauce

1 teaspoon Worcestershire sauce

1 teaspoon fresh chopped green onions

12 brioche buns (or hamburger buns of choice)

Butter (for the buns)

OPTIONAL TOPPINGS:

Colby Jack cheese slices

Canned pineapple slices, drained

Red onions, sliced

Lettuce

Barbecue sauce

DIRECTIONS:

1. In a large bowl, combine the beef, egg, and cream, creating a moist mixture.

2. Add the bread crumbs, garlic powder, onion powder, lemon pepper seasoning, soy sauce, Worcestershire sauce, and green onions. Combine thoroughly. (At this point you can remove a tiny piece of the meat to cook over the stove and test for taste. If it's smackin', then keep it moving with larger patties.)

3. Using gloved hands, create 12 patties, each about ¼ inch thick.

4. Cook on a grill, skillet, or griddle on high heat for 3–4 minutes on each side. The patty should be browned and cooked through to the center.

5. Top each patty with a slice of cheese, if using, and set aside to let it melt.

6. Melt a dab of butter in a pan over medium heat and toast the buns in batches until golden and crisp on the insides. Add butter to the pan as needed.

7. On the grill or in a grill pan over high heat, heat the pineapple, if using, for 30 seconds on each side, just long enough to get nice grill marks without losing too much juice.

Recipe Continues

8. Place each patty on a bottom bun and top with the pineapple, onion, lettuce, and barbecue sauce, if using.

9. Finish the masterpiece with the top bun and enjoy!

Pro tip: Keep your ground beef as cold as possible until you're ready to cook it. *Do not* leave your meat out to get to room temperature before cooking, giving harmful bacteria a chance to grow. Also try not to work it with your hands excessively; 3–5 minutes is plenty of time. The more you grind and mix, the more fats are leaving the patty and sticking to your hands, and *fat is flavor*.

CHAPTER SEVEN

SALADS DRESSED TO IMPRESS

Sure, there's a chance you can buy one bottle of salad dressing and it will be cheaper than the ingredients listed in these recipes. But a budget book should be more than just "the cheapest option." It should also highlight the most sustainable options. We waste so much food. I can't tell you how many times I have thrown out a bottle of salad dressing after it reached its expiration date. This chapter covers the basics of salad dressings, so you don't have to settle for a store-bought bottle you don't really love or won't use more than once. Additionally, almost each dressing is paired with its perfect partner. These salads are tried and true, and they bring out the best in each dressing. I know I keep pushing creativity, but it's so important when learning to love cooking. I don't want to just push my favorites on you without giving you freedom to make each creation your own. I want each recipe to represent who you are, even down to the way you clothe your lettuce.

CLASSIC VINAIGRETTE

Honestly, and please don't judge (this is a safe space, remember?), I used to dislike vinaigrette dressing. It was tangy, light, earthy, and I felt so strange dipping my lettuce leaves in it. Unfortunately for me, my husband loves it. He will take a good vinaigrette over any of the creamy stuff I prefer any day. He suggested (either that or he tricked me in my own kitchen) I make my own vinaigrette from scratch. I was hesitant. I didn't like the store-bought stuff, why would I like my own? Still, I did the research, created a recipe, and, lo and behold, was hooked. I have since found a love for the store-bought stuff too, but this recipe speaks to my heart. It's something I couldn't find in a preservative-filled and store-bought bottle, and I definitely won't forget about it in the back of my fridge.

PREP TIME: 5 MINUTES ❤ **YIELD:** 2 CUPS

INGREDIENTS:

¾ cup olive oil

½ cup red wine vinegar

2 tablespoons Dijon mustard

2 tablespoons honey

1½ teaspoons minced garlic

2 tablespoons fresh cilantro (or 2 teaspoons dried)

1 tablespoon fresh parsley (or 1 teaspoon dried)

¼ teaspoon salt

¼ teaspoon ground black pepper

DIRECTIONS:

1. Combine the oil, vinegar, mustard, honey, and garlic in a food processor or blender.
2. Stir in the cilantro, parsley, salt, and pepper and serve.

Pro tip: This recipe can be tweaked in so many ways. You can choose from a variety of vinegars, whichever you fancy. You can also add red pepper flakes, switch out the fresh or dried herbs, and even use different flavored honeys.

Here's a helpful list of suitable vinegars in order from most acidic to least acidic:

1. Red wine vinegar
2. Tarragon vinegar
3. White wine vinegar
4. Balsamic vinegar
5. Fruit vinegar

PERFECT VINAIGRETTE SALAD PAIRING

PREP TIME: 5 MINUTES ♥ **SERVES:** 2

INGREDIENTS:

2 cups shredded rainbow Swiss chard

2 cups shredded kale, stems removed

$\frac{1}{4}$ cup sunflower seeds

$\frac{1}{2}$ cup blueberries

$\frac{1}{4}$ cup glazed pecans

Classic Vinaigrette (page 101)

DIRECTIONS:

1. In each salad bowl, mix together 1 cup of the chard and 1 cup of the kale.

2. Top with half of each of the sunflower seeds, blueberries, and pecans.

3. Drizzle the Classic Vinaigrette over the salad and enjoy.

CLASSIC (JULIUS) CAESAR DRESSING

I asked my husband for ideas on a fun name to title this Caesar dressing recipe. We had a belly-aching laugh when he blurted out, "Julius Greens." We laughed harder when he explained his thinking behind his cleverly created title: "I thought you could call it Julius Greens like a play on Julius Caesar. You know the ape from *Planet of the Apes*? I figured apes would be herbivores and would probably enjoy a nice salad." There truly is never a dull moment in our home. Regardless of the name, I've seen this particular salad plated at least ten different ways. With chicken and without. With lettuce leaves shredded and with lettuce leaves whole like boats holding their Caesar-dressed passengers. However you decide to plate it, and whatever you decide to call it, dress it with this recipe.

PREP TIME: 5 MINUTES ❤ **YIELD:** 2 CUPS OR ENOUGH FOR 10 SALADS

INGREDIENTS:

1 cup mayonnaise

½ cup grated Parmesan cheese

1 lemon

1½ teaspoons Worcestershire sauce

1½ teaspoons Dijon mustard

1 teaspoon capers

1 teaspoon minced garlic

½ teaspoon salt

½ teaspoon ground black pepper

DIRECTIONS:

1. Put the mayonnaise and Parmesan cheese in a blender.
2. Roll the lemon on your countertop until it is slightly squishy. Cut the lemon in half and remove the seeds.
3. Squeeze the juice from each lemon half into the blender.
4. Add the remaining ingredients and blend on high for 30 seconds to 1 minute.

> **Pro tip:** This dressing is so versatile. Use it to coat your chicken wings, spread on a burger bun, or sub for mayonnaise in potato salad!

PERFECT (JULIUS) CAESAR SALAD PAIRING

PREP TIME: 2 MINUTES ❤ **SERVES:** 4 AS A SIDE

INGREDIENTS:

4 romaine lettuce leaves*

1 cup cooked, shredded chicken

½ cup croutons

Classic (Julius) Caesar Dressing (page 105)

* **Note:** The leaves will act like a boat for your toppings, so be careful to preserve their shape.

DIRECTIONS:

1. Spread ¼ cup of the chicken in each lettuce boat.

2. Top each boat with a quarter of the croutons.

3. Drizzle each boat with the Classic (Julius) Caesar Dressing and serve.

CLASSIC RANCH DRESSING

I believe this was voted America's number-one salad dressing. The appeal is duly noted. We eat this stuff on everything: burgers, veggies, chips, chicken, pizza, french fries, and more. You can find ranch dressing on virtually every menu everywhere. So many people love this stuff, it amazes me how few of us actually make it ourselves. There's not a chance that the bottled stuff is better or fresher than what you're about to whip up in your kitchen. Feeling adventurous? I promise you: One try is all it will take to hook you on the best ranch you've ever had in your life. Pour this dressing over your favorite salads, or use it as a dip for your favorite veggies or pizza (if you're one of those, no judgment here!).

PREP TIME: 5 MINUTES ♥ **YIELD:** 2½ CUPS

INGREDIENTS:

1 cup buttermilk

½ cup sour cream

¼ cup mayonnaise

2 teaspoons freeze-dried dill weed
(or 1 tablespoon fresh dill weed)

2 teaspoons freeze-dried chives (or 1 tablespoon fresh chopped chives)

1 teaspoon minced garlic

1 teaspoon fresh-squeezed lemon juice

¼ teaspoon salt

¼ teaspoon ground black pepper

DIRECTIONS:

1. Toss all the ingredients into a blender and let those blades of steel have a go at it for about 30 seconds to 1 minute (we love a good toss and blend recipe!). Store in your fridge for up to one week. That is, of course, if it hasn't been devoured by then.

LEMON-GARLIC-INFUSED OLIVE OIL

I love olive oil. My past self said, "Whoa, Lexy, that's kind of a weird thing to be passionate about." So I looked in the mirror and said, "Is it really, though?" Olive oil is an extremely versatile ingredient. Sure, it has many purposes. But also, when used right, it has the ability to give a dish a level of sophistication and deliciousness that it just didn't have before. My dream is to travel to Italy and get fresher-than-fresh-pressed olive oil. I can't wait to experience it the way it was meant to be experienced. Until then, I'll settle for amazing recipes like this one—a recipe that makes plain lettuce leaves look and taste amazing.

PREP TIME: 5 MINUTES ❤ **COOK TIME:** 5 MINUTES ❤ **REST TIME:** 1 HOUR ❤ **YIELD:** 2 CUPS

INGREDIENTS:

2 cups olive oil

Zest of 1 lemon, peeled (for flavor)

3 garlic cloves, crushed

2 fresh rosemary sprigs

DIRECTIONS:

1. Pour the oil into a nonstick pot and add the lemon zest, garlic, and rosemary. Warm over low heat for 5 minutes. Make sure your pan is not hot enough to actually cook the oil. Make it just hot enough to infuse the aromatics.

2. Transfer to an airtight container. (We use a mason jar with a twist top for this.)

3. Let sit for 1 hour. When you're ready to store, this will last in the fridge for one week. (Don't leave it at room temperature, to avoid the risk of botulism.)

Pro tip: Love this recipe? Try pouring it onto a plate and topping with as much grated Parmesan cheese as you like. Then use it as a dip for bread.

PERFECT LEMON-GARLIC-INFUSED OLIVE OIL SALAD PAIRING

PREP TIME: 2 MINUTES ❤ **SERVES:** 2

INGREDIENTS:

3 cups shredded iceberg lettuce

½ cup basil leaves, chiffonade

½ cup cherry or grape tomatoes, halved

½ cup pitted olives

½ cup chopped anchovies

½ cup grated Parmesan cheese

Lemon-Garlic-Infused Olive Oil (page 110)

DIRECTIONS:

1. Place 1½ cups of the lettuce in each bowl.
2. Add half of each of the basil, tomatoes, and olives to each bowl and mix together.
3. Sprinkle half of each of the anchovies and Parmesan on top of each bowl.
4. Finish with the Lemon-Garlic-Infused Olive Oil.

Round of Applause

If my play on words didn't quite land, this section is all about the appetizers. Some might use the recipes in the next chapter for entertaining and others for mid-day munching. The more playful among you might end your night here, opting to offer one or a combo of these apps as a light dinner alternative. Whatever the occasion (or hunger motivation), you're getting a well-rounded collection of recipes proven to satisfy your cravings whenever they strike.

CHAPTER EIGHT

PARTY PLEASERS!

(APPETIZERS FOR ALL OCCASIONS)

I am a hostess at heart. If you watch the TV show Friends as often as I do, then you've probably associated yourself with one of the characters. I am most definitely a Monica. I love the episode where she bakes cookies and fans the sweet aroma to her friends across the hall, luring them to her apartment. She did this to satiate her need to be the hostess of all hostesses. That is me. If I invite you over for a party, game night, or just a chill hangout, I will have food prepared the second you walk through my door. Another not-so-great trait of mine: I tend to overdo, like, everything. Got a hankering for tacos? I will buy three different kinds of meat and marinate them in three separate sauces. I'll make guacamole, pico de gallo, and corn and flour tortillas, and create an out-of-this-world taco bar. I have come to accept that it's just the way I am. But don't worry: You don't have to do all that. Sometimes you just need some go-to appetizers that are easy to whip up for your guests. Behold! Here are my favorite apps for any occasion, made with minimal effort and mouth-watering flavors.

MOZZARELLA MONKEY BREAD

If you've read this glorious book from cover to cover, then you've seen the breakfast version of this delicious monkey bread. The gist of both dishes is the same: easy, hands-off, and fun to eat. However, this version has one major difference. Did someone say pull-apart cheese?! Your guests will have a blast pulling apart this bread and chatting while you finish cooking up your main course. The hole in the middle of the bread is the perfect spot for a bowl of marinara for dipping.

PREP TIME: 20 MINUTES ♥ **COOK TIME:** 25 MINUTES ♥ **SERVES:** 6–8

INGREDIENTS:

Two 16-ounce cans jumbo biscuits (8 count each)

Oil or butter, for greasing

8 ounces fresh mozzarella, cut into 32 chunks about $\frac{1}{2}$ inch each

2 cups grated Parmesan cheese

2 tablespoons Italian seasoning

1 tablespoon freeze-dried chives

1 tablespoon salt

$1\frac{1}{2}$ teaspoons ground black pepper

1 stick ($\frac{1}{2}$ cup) butter, melted

Pro tip: Place a piece of pepperoni inside each biscuit ball along with the mozzarella and enjoy a pull-apart pizza appetizer that your friends can dip in marinara.

DIRECTIONS:

1. Preheat the oven to 350°F. Grease a Bundt pan.
2. Remove the biscuits from the cans and cut each biscuit in half.
3. Place a chunk of mozzarella in the center of each biscuit half and fold the dough over the cheese.
4. Roll the dough around the mozzarella chunk, pinching and palm-rolling until the cheese is completely enclosed. Repeat with the rest of the biscuit pieces.
5. Place the Parmesan, Italian seasoning, chives, salt, and pepper in a zip-top bag. Seal and shake to mix.
6. Place the biscuit pieces in the bag and shake to coat.
7. Transfer the biscuit pieces into the prepared Bundt pan.
8. In a bowl, combine the remaining Parmesan mixture with the butter and pour over the biscuits.
9. Bake in the oven for 25 minutes, or until the biscuits are golden brown and have doubled in size.
10. Turn the bread out from the pan onto a plate and serve.

SPICED HONEY BUTTER

Yes, this is a recipe for butter. I promise you: If you make this, everyone will ask you for the recipe. There is nothing more laid back than putting out some sliced bread and letting your guests go to town on a tub full of the best butter they've ever tasted. I can't take all the credit; I was inspired by the famous Texas Roadhouse butter. I want to say mine is better, so I'll say it: Mine is better. Don't believe me? Guess you'll have to make this recipe and decide for yourself. Serve this with rolls, crescents, or any bread you prefer.

PREP TIME: 10 MINUTES ❤ **CONSUMPTION TIME:** 2 SECONDS ❤ **YIELD:** ABOUT 1 CUP

INGREDIENTS:

2 sticks (1 cup) butter, softened*

1 cup powdered sugar

1 tablespoon honey

1 teaspoon vanilla extract

½ teaspoon almond extract

2 teaspoons ground cinnamon

½ teaspoon ground cardamom

¼ teaspoon salt

* **Note:** Make sure your butter is *softened,* not melted. Melted butter will not hold up, and the consistency of the butter will be negatively impacted.

DIRECTIONS:

1. Start by whipping together the butter and powdered sugar for 3–4 minutes. Start slow and work the mixing speed up as the minutes go by. This butter should be lighter than air.

2. Gently fold in all the remaining ingredients. The butter should be silky smooth and light brown in color, with darker brown flecks.

Pro tip: While you can make this by hand with a whisk or fork, a stand or hand mixer will give you a fluffier consistency much faster.

CAPRESE CHICKEN SKEWERS

Balsamic vinegar, chicken, and fresh mozzarella. Mmmmm … This recipe's a no-brainer. It's clinically proven to cure awkward silences at any function. (No, seriously. I mean, if you're not familiar with my sense of humor at this point in the book, then there's no way you've been reading my little stories. So you probably aren't reading me explaining myself right now, either. Hmm, there's some real freedom in knowing you can write whatever you want when no one's paying attention. Dirty dishes, if you can hear me, not a fan.) Anyway, no one will care about awkward silences when these bad boys come out because everyone will be too busy stuffing their mouths.

COOK TIME: 12 MINUTES ❤ **ASSEMBLY TIME:** 10 MINUTES ❤ **YIELD:** 12 SKEWERS

INGREDIENTS:

1 tablespoon olive oil

1 pound sliced chicken breasts

¼ cup balsamic vinegar

1 teaspoon garlic powder

1 teaspoon onion powder

1 teaspoon dried oregano

1 teaspoon honey

2 cups spinach

16 ounces mozzarella balls

36 grape tomatoes

Pro tip: Do not try to make these on the grill by assembling first. The mozzarella will melt, and it will be a mess. Instead, cook the chicken on the grill separately and then assemble as instructed.

DIRECTIONS:

1. Heat a skillet for 2 minutes over high heat. Drizzle the oil in the pan.
2. Sear the chicken for 1 minute and flip, then sear the other side for 1 minute. The chicken should have a nice golden-brown color but still be raw inside.
3. Combine the vinegar, garlic powder, onion powder, oregano, and honey in a small bowl and pour into the skillet.
4. Reduce the heat to low and cook for 7 minutes, or until the liquid has thickened. Remove from the heat.
5. Roll the chicken in the sauce to coat and start assembling the skewers.
6. You can assemble these however your heart desires, but here's how I do it: 1 piece of chicken followed by 2 pieces of spinach (folded and pierced on each end), 1 piece of cheese, 1 tomato, 1 piece of chicken, 2 pieces of spinach, 1 tomato, 1 piece of cheese, and 1 final piece of chicken.
7. Place on a serving tray and eat immediately.

MONTE CRISTO CRESCENT ROLLS

As far as I'm concerned, Monte Cristo sandwiches are the fanciest on Earth. I'm sure they're not the only fancy sandwiches in town. After all, there are cucumber sandwiches (which I still don't understand). And sure, there are six other continents whose sandwich situations I have yet to explore. Nonetheless, the first time I had a Monte Cristo sandwich, my mouth felt like it exploded. Jam … with cheese and meat … deep fried? Culinary euphoria. I've made this sandwich a bunch of different ways. This recipe is budget friendly (per usual) and so incredibly easy. It is not deep-fried, so the cleanup is a dream. It's everything you would want in an easy, warm-up meal from the comfort of your own home.

PREP TIME: 10 MINUTES ♥ **COOK TIME:** 20 MINUTES ♥ **SERVES:** 6–12

INGREDIENTS:

SANDWICHES:

Two 8-ounce cans crescent rolls (8 count each)

½ pound sliced honey ham

½ pound sliced smoked turkey

6 slices Swiss cheese

SAUCE:

12 ounces (1½ cups) frozen raspberries

½ cup granulated sugar

½ cup plus 2 tablespoons water

1 tablespoon cornstarch

Powdered sugar

> **Pro tip:** You can also fry these in canola oil for 3–4 minutes for a more authentic experience.

DIRECTIONS:

FOR THE SANDWICHES:

1. Preheat the oven to 350°F.
2. Remove and separate the crescent rolls and place on an ungreased baking sheet.
3. On the largest section of each unrolled crescent roll (about a quarter of the total surface), layer half a piece of ham (folded), half a slice of Swiss cheese, and half a piece of turkey (folded).
4. Roll the crescent and fold the sides over the top of the roll to secure the stuffing. Repeat with the remaining rolls.
5. Bake in the oven for 15 minutes, or until golden brown and the cheese is melted.

FOR THE SAUCE:

1. Mix the raspberries, granulated sugar, and ½ cup of the water in a saucepan over low heat and simmer until the sugar is fully dissolved, about 8 minutes.
2. In a separate bowl, mix the remaining 2 tablespoons water with the cornstarch to create a slurry.
3. Pour the slurry into the raspberry sauce and simmer for an additional 5 minutes.
4. Remove from the heat and let stand 5 minutes before serving.

TO SERVE:

1. Sprinkle the sandwiches with powdered sugar and serve with the sauce.

CRAZY CHEESY FLATBREAD

Let's be real here: Flatbread is pretty much pizza. And I have yet to find a single soul who doesn't like pizza! So theoretically, this recipe should be a huge hit. The best part is you can switch this up however you want. Add toppings that feel more you, or put out a bunch of toppings and have your guests go nuts loading it up. They'll be that much more excited when it's time to dig in, knowing they contributed. (Best part is that if your guests make this, then you don't have to!)

PREP TIME: 10 MINUTES ❤ **COOK TIME:** 20 MINUTES ❤ **SERVES:** 6–12

INGREDIENTS:

1 can refrigerated pizza dough, such as Pillsbury Pizza Crust

1 cup pesto

$\frac{1}{4}$ cup chopped grape tomatoes

$\frac{1}{2}$ cup spinach

8 ounces pearled fresh mozzarella balls

4 ounces goat cheese

1 teaspoon Italian seasoning

1 teaspoon salt

2 tablespoons olive oil

DIRECTIONS:

1. Preheat the oven to 350°F. Lightly flour a baking sheet.
2. Unroll the pizza dough on the baking sheet.
3. Spread the pesto over the rectangular-shaped dough.
4. Top with the tomatoes, spinach, mozzarella, goat cheese, Italian seasoning, and salt.
5. Drizzle the oil on top.
6. Bake in the oven for 12–15 minutes, until the cheese is melted and the crust is golden brown. Remove from the oven.
7. Make six cuts widthwise and one cut lengthwise for twelve slices of flatbread.

Pro tip: This is a fun meal to make with kids. Cut the pizza dough in half and let them go bananas building mini pizzas of their choice. My kids like to top this with canned pizza sauce, shredded mozzarella, and lots of pepperoni slices.

Dinner's Ready!

There's nothing like a delicious meal at the end of the day. Some days end better than others, but I firmly believe a proper meal can fix almost anything. When I'm sad, I want good food. When I'm happy, I want good food. Either way, I want good food. Dinner is the last chance in the day for us to nourish our bodies. When I started to think of it that way, a quick grab of fast food on my way home just didn't cut it anymore. I owe myself a hearty meal. No time to make an elaborate meal? No worries. I've added a chapter of meals that can be ready at your table in thirty minutes. Don't know how to properly cook the basic meats in your fridge? I got you. This section also has a list of the most commonly accessible meats and how to cook them perfectly, every time. I even added some splendid ideas to take the stress out of figuring out what side dish to pair with your dinner's main character. There's a little something for everyone and every need in this section. Because this is your last chance at making your day worthwhile, and you deserve it.

PERFECT PROTEINS FROM LAND TO SEA

Most home cooks have ruined the star of their dish—the meat—at least once. It's so tragic. You work hard, decide to do a little self-care by cooking for yourself, and then bite into meat that's dry, tough, chewy, and bland. I'm not criticizing. I've been there too, and it's awful. I've been there so often, in fact, that I vowed to never completely destroy any other major protein in my kitchen. I devoted my energy to testing various cooking methods and perfecting cooking/baking/frying times, so you don't have to face the tragedy of ruined meat. In this section, I charted the most popular meats, listing the proper cooking temperatures and a few other useful tips. I've included advice like proper internal temperature, perfect seasoning pairings, and recipes to put your newfound skills to the test. Don't sweat it, babe, I got your six!

CHAPTER NINE

THE PERFECT CHICKEN

Making the perfect chicken is no small feat. One time, I was so distraught after royally destroying a baked chicken, I took a pint of ice cream from the freezer, locked myself in my room, and ate the whole thing in one sitting. I admit that I can be a bit dramatic. (Just don't tell my husband that I agree with him on that one.) Not only did I waste my time, but I also wasted my money. I'm all about my budget, and nothing screams "budget ruined" like inedible food in the trash can. This chapter is specially designed to help you not be like me. This chapter has all the most important charts, notes, and tips to make sure your chicken comes out right every time. Need a little extra help deciding what to make with your protein? I added a few of my go-to recipes that will guarantee you can make a whole meal, including perfectly baked, fried, or sautéed chicken.

PERFECT PAIRINGS FOR CHICKEN:

Salt, pepper, garlic, onion, thyme, parsley, paprika, mushroom, rosemary, cheeses, creams (crème fraîche or heavy cream for sauces)

CHICKEN SEASONING TIPS

- My recipes have the seasonings measured out, but if you want to grab the reins and go rogue, that's great! Just try to add about 1 teaspoon of seasoning per ½ pound of chicken.

- Try to not layer more than three different seasonings outside of salt and pepper.
- Thoroughly rub the chicken with seasoning. Massage it in to make sure the chicken is evenly coated.
- Stuffing chicken with cream cheese is a great way to add extra moisture. Season the cream cheese beforehand to add extra flavor.
- Soaking chicken in buttermilk is a great way to tenderize it. (I've found it helps the seasonings cling to the chicken better too.)
- When frying, make sure you season both the frying flour and the chicken.

TYPES OF CHICKEN	BAKE	SAUTÉ	FRY	INTERNAL TEMPERATURE
WINGS	30 minutes at 375°F	Not recommended	8–11 minutes	165°F
BREASTS	25 minutes at 375°F (boneless) 35 minutes at 375°F (bone-in)	4–5 minutes on each side over medium-high heat	15–18 minutes	165°F
LEGS	40–45 minutes at 375°F	Not recommended	12–15 minutes	165°F
THIGHS	25–30 minutes at 375°F	10–12 minutes	14–16 minutes	165°F
TENDERLOINS	15–20 minutes at 350°F	2–3 minutes per side over medium-high heat	5–8 minutes	165°F
WHOLE CHICKEN	23 minutes per pound: 425°F for first 23 minutes; 350°F for the remaining time	Not recommended	Not recommended	165°F

CHICKEN COOKING TIPS

When baking chicken, use a shallow pan or sheet pan to help regulate airflow and speed up the cooking process.

When frying, heat your oil (canola, vegetable, grapeseed, and peanut oil are all great options) over medium-low heat for 20 minutes to get it hot without burning it.

To test the oil, sprinkle a pinch of flour into the pot. If the flour crackles and bubbles, the oil is hot enough to begin frying. Likewise, you can stick the end of a wooden spoon into the grease; if small bubbles form around it, you are ready to go.

It can be difficult to know when your chicken is done frying. There are a few tricks I've learned that will help along your way.

- One option is to listen. Take note of the loud sound your chicken makes when it starts frying. It will lower in volume when it's done cooking.

- Another way you can tell if your chicken is done frying is to observe its buoyancy. The higher it floats, the more done it is.

- The most foolproof way is to measure the internal temperature of your chicken. Stick a thermometer in the thickest part of the chicken. If it reads 165°F, your chicken is fully cooked.

- If you don't have a thermometer you can remove one piece from the fryer, make a small incision in the largest part of the chicken, and turn your knife sideways to expose the flesh. The meat should look white and moist.

When sautéing, after one side is cooked and you're ready to flip, reduce the heat to low, cover the pan with a lid, and cook the second side for an additional minute. This will keep your chicken juicy and cooked evenly.

Let's get into it!

CLUCKIN' GOOD WINGS

The best wings I've ever ordered came from the West Side of Chicago; the best wings that were ever made for me came from my grandma's house on the South Side. As you can see, both of the best wing dishes I've ever had come from the greatest city of all time: Chicago. Unfortunately, I hate the weather there and have since moved. The place where I live now does not have good wings—at all. I didn't realize how good I had it until it was gone. So, I had to learn to make wings myself! Try this recipe and rank it; this ended up in my top five. I like to serve these with fries.

PREP TIME: 10 MINUTES ♥ **COOK TIME:** 5–6 MINUTES PER BATCH ♥ **SERVES:** 1–2

INGREDIENTS:

6 chicken wings

1 quart canola or vegetable oil

3 cups flour

2 tablespoons ground black pepper

2 tablespoons Lawry's Seasoned Salt

2 tablespoons onion powder

2 tablespoons garlic powder

1 tablespoon cornstarch

Pro tip: Buy a bag of frozen fries and fry them for about 10 minutes in the same preheated oil you used to fry your chicken. This will add flavor to the fries.

DIRECTIONS:

1. Heat the oil in a frying pot or deep pan until hot, about 5 minutes.
2. Place the flour in a large bowl and season with 1 tablespoon each of pepper, Lawry's, onion powder, and garlic powder.
3. Add the cornstarch and stir until combined.
4. In a small bowl, stir together the remaining tablespoon each of pepper, Lawry's, onion powder, and garlic powder. Rub the seasoning thoroughly into the chicken.
5. Drop the seasoned chicken into the flour mixture and coat well.
6. Tap off any excess flour and carefully place the chicken in the oil.
7. Cook for 5–6 minutes, until cooked through (165°F).
8. Remove from the oil and place on a wire rack or a plate lined with a paper towel to drain excess oil.

CREAM CHEESE–STUFFED BAKED CHICKEN AND VEGGIE MEDLEY

This. Recipe. Right. Here! I may as well be working in the office because this is a *staple*. The chicken comes out juicy every time, and it is so easy to make. Sometimes we eat it with rice, but you don't have to. It's a great meal to bring to a potluck. You can make a huge batch of this dish quickly, easily, and affordably.

PREP TIME: 15 MINUTES ❤ **COOK TIME:** 25 MINUTES ❤ **SERVES:** 3–6

INGREDIENTS:

2 tablespoons olive oil

1 red pepper, sliced

1 green pepper, sliced

1 yellow pepper, sliced

1 zucchini, sliced

1 yellow squash, sliced

4 chicken breasts

2 tablespoons salt

2 tablespoons lemon pepper seasoning

4 ounces cream cheese

4 tablespoons butter

Pro tip: The extra juices that you'll find in this pan taste great when poured on rice!

DIRECTIONS:

1. Preheat the oven to 375°F.
2. Drizzle 1 tablespoon of the oil in a 9 x 13-inch baking pan. Add the peppers, zucchini, and squash to the pan. Season with 1 tablespoon each of the salt and lemon pepper seasoning.
3. Using a sharp knife, cut a pocket in a chicken breast. Start your cut ¼ inch from the edge of the chicken and make an incision that stretches to the other side of the breast, leaving ¼ inch on the opposite end as well. Gently deepen the incision with your knife to the back of the chicken breast, creating a pocket that ends ¼ inch from the back of the breast. Repeat for the other three breasts.
4. Drizzle the chicken breasts with the remaining tablespoon oil and massage well.
5. Divide the cream cheese evenly among each chicken breast and firmly spread into each pocket.
6. Season with the remaining tablespoon each of the salt and lemon pepper seasoning and place in the pan on top of the veggies.
7. Chop the butter into small pieces and place on top of the chicken.
8. Bake in the oven for 25 minutes, or until the chicken is cooked through (165°F) and the tops are slightly browned.

HOT HONEY SAUTÉED CHICKEN

I'm a sucker for Chinese food. While I'm not a huge fan of the commercialized joints, I do thoroughly enjoy General Tso's chicken. This recipe is my attempt to satisfy my Chinese food cravings while spending half the amount and waiting a quarter of the time.

PREP TIME: 5 MINUTES ❤ **COOK TIME:** 20 MINUTES ❤ **SERVES:** 3–6

INGREDIENTS:

4 cups water

2 cups rice

1 teaspoon salt

1 teaspoon ground black pepper

4 tablespoons butter

2 pounds chicken tenders

2 tablespoons cornstarch

1 teaspoon chili powder

½ teaspoon red pepper flakes

1 tablespoon minced garlic

¼ cup honey

3 tablespoons soy sauce

2 tablespoons white or red wine vinegar

Sesame seeds (for garnish; optional)

Fresh chopped chives (for garnish; optional)

Rice (for serving)

DIRECTIONS:

1. In a saucepan over high heat, bring the water and rice to a boil.
2. Reduce the heat to low and add the salt, pepper, and 1 tablespoon of the butter.
3. Cover and cook for 15–20 minutes, until the water is absorbed and the rice is fluffy when forked.
4. Meanwhile, place the cornstarch in a dish and dredge the chicken in it.
5. Combine the chili powder, red pepper flakes, garlic, honey, soy sauce, and vinegar in a small bowl and set aside.
6. Melt the remaining 3 tablespoons butter in a skillet over medium-high heat and add the chicken. Cook for 3 minutes on one side, or until browned, and flip.
7. Pour the sauce into the pan and cook for another 3–4 minutes on medium-low, until the chicken is cooked through (165°F).
8. Sprinkle with the sesame seeds and chives, if using, and serve with rice.

> **Budget tip:** Freshen your leftovers by adding your cold, dried-out rice to a skillet with a few tablespoons of canola oil. Fry and add 1–2 tablespoons soy sauce to make fried rice.

CHAPTER TEN

THE PERFECT FISH

There are many different kinds of fish. I could write a whole separate book in detail about each of the varieties. Unfortunately, I am only contracted for one book at the moment. So, I decided to do a little research and give you tips for the three most commonly purchased and used cuts of fish. We're going to look at all things salmon, tilapia, and tuna in this chapter. I've filled this chapter with charts, tips, seasoning combos, and recipes that best represent each of the different catches of the day!

TYPES OF FISH	INTERNAL TEMPERATURE	BEST COOKING METHOD	BEST SEASONINGS
SALMON	130–135°F	Bake covered in foil for 25 minutes at 350°F	Bay leaf, basil, garlic, thyme, shallots, parsley, lemon, Old Bay, salt, pepper
TILAPIA	145°F	Sauté on medium-high heat for 2–3 minutes per side	Salt, pepper, lemon pepper, lime, lemon, parsley, fennel
TUNA	115°F	Sear in a heated pan for 2–2.5 minutes on each side, and let rest 10 minutes	Lime, soy sauce, ginger, garlic, chives, shallots, sesame seeds

FISH PREP/COOKING TIPS:

THAWING FROZEN FISH

You can thaw frozen fish a few ways.

- Thaw fish in the fridge for 6–8 hours or overnight. This is the easiest method and preserves the integrity of the flesh the best.
- Place the fish in a resealable plastic bag and set in a bowl full of cold water. This method will take 2–3 hours.
- The fastest method is to defrost in the microwave in 30-second intervals. (I do not recommend this method.) Be careful when trying this method because you risk heating the fish too much in certain spots and creating a temperature suitable for breeding bacteria.

SALMON

Properly cooked salmon is pale pink with a slightly brighter pink center. The flesh is moist and flaky.

When cooking salmon in a skillet, score the skin side by making hatch marks along the scales about ¼ inch thick. This will stop the salmon from curling in your pan and speed up cooking time.

Drizzle the pan with 1 tablespoon olive oil and heat before adding your salmon fillet.

Cook the salmon until the bright pink flesh is pale pink three-quarters of the way up the sides of the fillet. Then flip and cook for an additional 2–3 minutes.

When cooking salmon in the oven, slice fresh pieces of lemon and place them, along with ½ tablespoon butter, alongside every 2 inches of fillet. You can add aromatics like rosemary, bay leaf, and basil to the tops of the salmon and cover with foil for a deliciously juicy and perfectly flavored fillet every time.

TILAPIA

When cooking tilapia, pay attention to the color and texture of the flesh. Perfectly cooked tilapia will be slightly opaque, flaky, and visibly moist.

TUNA

When cooking tuna steaks, use steaks that are at least 1-inch thick.

Tuna should be eaten with a bright purple center and seared outsides.

Tuna becomes crumbly and bitter, with a slight metallic taste, when it's overcooked. *Do not overcook this fillet!*

The thicker your tuna steak, the more room you'll have for slight errors in cooking times.

Budget tip: Canned tuna is a great cheap alternative to use in many salmon recipes. Try it in my Tuscan Salmon and Spinach Manicotti on page 163.

**Quick One-Sheet Salmon,
page 144**

QUICK ONE-SHEET SALMON

Salmon is so good for you—a great source of protein and healthy fats. It is also one of the only meats my kid will eat besides chicken nuggets. Who would have thought that someone like me (who loves to cook and spends half her day in the kitchen) would end up with the world's pickiest child? Nonetheless, this recipe is perfect and happily feeds the family every time.

PREP TIME: 10 MINUTES ♥ **COOK TIME:** 25 MINUTES ♥ **SERVES:** 4

INGREDIENTS:

2 pounds salmon

4 teaspoons Old Bay seasoning

2 tablespoons butter

1 lemon, sliced

¼ cup basil, chopped

2 pounds asparagus, trimmed

4 rosemary sprigs

DIRECTIONS:

1. Preheat the oven to 350°F.
2. Rinse the salmon and cut into four equal fillets. If the salmon is frozen and individually packaged, thaw before cooking. (See page 142 for thawing tips.)
3. Tear four pieces of foil long enough to completely wrap each fillet.
4. Place the fillets on the foil and sprinkle each with 1 teaspoon of the Old Bay seasoning. Top each with a lemon slice. Add ½ tablespoon of the butter to the top of the lemon slice. Sprinkle each fillet with 1 tablespoon of the basil.
5. Separate the asparagus into four equal portions and place one in each foil pocket, along with a rosemary sprig.
6. Seal the foil pockets and place on a baking sheet.
7. Bake in the oven for 25 minutes, or until cooked through.
8. Transfer the contents of the foil pockets to plates and serve.

Simple Crusted Tuna Steaks,
page 146

SIMPLE CRUSTED TUNA STEAKS

This recipe is not something I make often. Good tuna steaks run a little pricier than I like to spend, but they are delicious. Not everyone's budget is the same, so I thought I would include a recipe that really highlights how to cook this tuna to perfection but also shows ingredients that complement this protein so well.

PREP TIME: 10 MINUTES ❤ **COOK TIME:** 15 MINUTES ❤ **SERVES:** 2

INGREDIENTS:

32 ounces tuna steaks (or 2 steaks, 1 pound each)

2 teaspoons salt

2 teaspoons ground black pepper

1 tablespoon olive oil

½ cup bread crumbs

1 teaspoon freeze-dried chives

½ teaspoon cayenne pepper

½ teaspoon dried thyme

2 tablespoons mayonnaise

1 green pepper, thinly sliced

1 red pepper, thinly sliced

1 cup arugula, packed

1 tablespoon butter

DIRECTIONS:

1. Season each side of the tuna steaks with ½ teaspoon each of the salt and black pepper.
2. Heat a skillet over high heat and drizzle in the oil.
3. While the skillet and oil are heating, combine the bread crumbs, chives, cayenne, and thyme. Mix well.
4. Spread 1 tablespoon of the mayo on one side of each steak and dip in the bread crumbs, coating well.
5. Place the steaks in the heated skillet, bread crumb side down, and sear for 3 minutes. The bread crumbs should be golden brown and crusted over. You should be able to see that the steaks have cooked about a quarter to half the way up the sides.
6. Flip each steak and cook for an additional minute.
7. Transfer the steaks to a plate, breaded side up, and let rest for 10 minutes.
8. Turn the heat down to medium-low. Cook the peppers, arugula, and butter in the pan for 10 minutes.
9. To serve, place half of the veggies on each plate and top with a steak, crusted side up.

Tongue-Tingling Tilapia Tacos,
page 148

TONGUE-TINGLING TILAPIA TACOS

Fish tacos are not something I grew up eating, but that did not stop me from growing to love them. Tilapia takes mere minutes to cook, making this dish probably one of the fastest in this book to prepare. I wanted to focus on complementary flavors, so, I made a spicy, slightly tangy slaw to accompany this mild and buttery soft fish. The slight crunch from the cabbage guarantees that the senses will be firing from all angles, leaving your taste buds tingly and satisfied.

PREP TIME: 10 MINUTES ❤ **COOK TIME:** 5 MINUTES ❤ **SERVES:** 4

INGREDIENTS:

2 pounds tilapia fillets

2 teaspoons salt, plus more for the slaw

2 teaspoons lemon pepper seasoning, plus more for the slaw

1 tablespoon olive oil

2 chipotle peppers in adobo, or 1¼ teaspoons of the adobo sauce from the can*

½ cup sour cream

1 tablespoon lime juice

1 tablespoon fresh chopped cilantro

3 cups shredded cabbage

8 tortillas

* **Note:** Using the chipotle peppers instead of their sauce will give you a spicier sauce because the seeds inside the peppers will also be incorporated. If your heart's desire is a spicier sauce, use 2 or 3 whole peppers to make the sour cream sauce. If you decide to use the adobo sauce instead of the actual peppers, simply combine the ingredients with a spoon.

DIRECTIONS:

1. Season the tilapia with the salt and lemon pepper seasoning and set aside.
2. Heat a skillet over medium heat until hot, about 1 minute.
3. Drizzle in the oil and swirl around the pan to coat.
4. Place the fillets in the pan and cook for 2 minutes on each side.
5. Transfer to a bowl and shred with a fork.
6. Blend the chipotle peppers with the sour cream, lime juice, and cilantro.
7. In a separate bowl, toss the chipotle sauce with the cabbage and season with salt and pepper to taste.
8. Heat the tortillas in a little oil in a pan over medium heat for 1 minute on each side, if desired.
9. Top each tortilla with the tilapia and slaw to serve.

Pro tip: Substitute mahi-mahi for tilapia and add a squeeze of fresh orange for a more elevated dish.

CHAPTER ELEVEN

THE PERFECT STEAK

If you like your steak well done, this chapter is not for you. Okay, I'm being dramatic again. There are still very helpful tips, charts, seasoning suggestions, and recipes in this chapter for you too. This book does not discriminate on your steak preferences (though I cannot say the same thing for myself). However you choose to cook it, and however you choose to eat it, this chapter is here to assist in all your efforts to make sure it will turn out perfect!

HIGH STEAKS FOR LOW BUDGETS

Because steak can be kind of pricey, the recipes listed have minimal and cheap side ingredients. Everything can be found at your local grocery store. My goal is to give you easy, budget-conscious meals that shine, even on special occasions. These recipes really let the steak be the star of the dish.

SEASONING TIPS

Steak needs very little seasoning. Most chefs only season steak with salt and pepper. If you are feeling fancy, you can throw a sprig of thyme or rosemary in the pan with your steak for a little extra flavor.

TAKING YOUR STEAK'S TEMPERATURE

I recommend investing in a meat thermometer and using this chart of the internal temperatures needed for your desired cook.

Rare	120°F
Medium-rare	130°F
Medium	140°F
Medium-well	150°F
Well-done	160°F

If your budget doesn't allow for a meat thermometer, the hand test will do. Check the doneness of your steak by comparing the firmness of your steak to the firmness of your palm as you connect the tip of your thumb to each of your other four fingers.

- Open your hand and touch your palm with the opposite hand's index finger. The firmness of your palm will be similar to that of a raw steak.
- Touch the tip of your thumb to same hand's index finger. The firmness of your palm will be similar to that of a rare steak.
- Touch the tip of your thumb to same hand's middle finger. The firmness of your palm will be similar to that of a medium-rare steak.
- Touch the tip of your thumb to same hand's ring finger. The firmness of your palm will be similar to that of a medium steak.
- Touch the tip of your thumb to same hand's pinky finger. The firmness of your palm will be similar to that of a well-done steak.

STEAK COOKING TIPS

1. Keep in mind that your steak will continue to cook while resting, with the temperature rising about 5–10 degrees. If you are aiming for a perfect medium, try taking your steak out at 130–135 degrees Fahrenheit. It's a good idea to let your steak rest for about the same amount of time it took to cook it.

2. While resting, not only is the steak still cooking, but the muscle is relaxing as the temperature drops. The result? The juiciest steak.

3. Cook your steak in grapeseed oil, which has a higher smoking point than olive oil.

4. Never cook a steak straight from the fridge. If your steak is cold, you'll have to cook it longer to get the inside to temp, which can lead to overcooking on the outside. Try to leave your steak on the counter for at least 20 minutes before placing it in the pan.

These tips apply to all cuts of steak, but there are certain things to know about specific cuts. I've listed the most popular here.

FILET MIGNON

Filet mignon comes from the tenderloin of the cow. The muscle is rarely worked so it is extremely tender. Although this cut is juicy, it lacks fat. It is really important to baste this with butter when cooking. You can also put a knob of butter on top of the steak while it rests.

- To cook filet mignon, heat a cast-iron or oven-safe skillet until smoking hot.
- Drizzle in a tablespoon of grapeseed oil and sear the filet for 2 minutes each on the top and bottom of the steak.
- Additionally, sear the sides for 1 minute each.
- Place the filet in an oven preheated to 350°F for 4–5 minutes, until the meat thermometer reads 130°F.
- Remove from the oven and set aside to rest for at least 8 minutes.

RIBEYE

Ribeye steak has the most marbling of the three cuts we are discussing in this book. Marbling is the lines of white or slightly pinkish fat that run throughout the muscle. Because ribeye has so much marbling, it is extremely flavorful and juicy. Imagine little pockets of buttery flavor weaved throughout your steak. As it cooks, the fat melts into the surrounding fibers. Make sure to give the fat cap (the chunk of fat on the side of your steak) a hard sear as well.

- To cook a ribeye steak, place it in a skillet, over high heat, in about a tablespoon of grapeseed oil.
- Cook for 3 minutes on one side, then flip it, add about 2 tablespoons butter, and cook for 3 minutes.
- As the butter melts, spoon the foamy butter over the steak. You can add in fresh aromatics and garlic at this time too. The flavors will seep into the butter and fuse with the steak as the butter gets spooned on top.
- Sear the fat cap for 1 minute.

NEW YORK STRIP

New York strip steak has less marbling than the ribeye but more than the filet. A trick to getting a perfect cook throughout the length of the steak is to cover it in plastic wrap and beat it with a meat tenderizer until it is even. Likewise, you can roll it with a small rolling pin.

- Cook this cut similar to the ribeye.
- Sear both sides for about 4 minutes.
- Baste with butter while the second side is searing.

SURF AND TURF WITH RIBEYE

Surf and turf is a classic West Coast dish and a great example of all the ways you can transform an idea. I have seen so many variations of this dish, and while there was so much more that could be done, I wanted to be real with you: I didn't create a budget book simply because I thought it would sell. This is my life. So I made a surf and turf that features epic flavors with epic savings.

PREP TIME: 10 MINUTES ❤ **COOK TIME:** 25 MINUTES ❤ **SERVES:** 2

INGREDIENTS:

2 ribeye steaks (each 1–1½ inch thick)

4 teaspoons salt

4 teaspoons ground black pepper

1 tablespoon grapeseed oil

4 tablespoons butter

½ cup grape tomatoes, cut in half

¼ red onion, thinly sliced

1 cup raw, cleaned, and deveined shrimp

2 teaspoons lemon pepper seasoning

1 teaspoon freeze-dried chives

2 tablespoons crumbled feta cheese

Pro tip: Try scoring the fat cap and rubbing with coarse salt before you begin cooking for a little extra flavor.

DIRECTIONS:

1. Heat an empty cast-iron or nonstick skillet over high heat until smoking hot.
2. Meanwhile, season each steak on each side with 1 teaspoon each of the salt and black pepper.
3. Drizzle the oil into the hot pan and lay the steaks down away from you.
4. Sear for 3 minutes and then flip.
5. Add the butter. Once the butter starts to foam, scoop it with a spoon and baste the steaks with it. Continue cooking and basting for 3 minutes.
6. Turn the steaks on their fat cap and sear for an additional 3 minutes. (The steak's fat cap is a thick strip of fat located on the side of the steak.) You can let the steaks rest on the side of the pan with the fat cap facing down or hold them with tongs.
7. Remove from the pan and place on a board or plate to rest.
8. Reduce the heat to low and add the tomatoes and onion to the same pan.*
9. Cook for about 5 minutes, until the tomatoes have broken down and the onions are soft.
10. Add the shrimp and cook for an additional 5 minutes.
11. Remove from the heat and add the lemon pepper seasoning and chives. Mix until combined.
12. Spoon the shrimp mixture on top of each steak. Top with the feta and serve.

*** Note:** You could remove some of the fat in the pan if you purchased a particularly fat, heavy piece of steak.

EASY-PEASY NEW YORK STRIP

New York strips are the first cut of steak I grew accustomed to. They are full of flavor and most times not quite as expensive as their cousin cuts. I use this to prove that cooking does not need to be complicated. You don't need a bunch of ingredients to make a great meal. This recipe is simply steak and potatoes. It's not what you have but what you do with it that counts.

PREP TIME: 5 MINUTES 💙 **COOK TIME:** 30 MINUTES 💙 **SERVES:** 2

INGREDIENTS:

3 potatoes, washed and cubed

4 tablespoons grapeseed oil

1 tablespoon salt

1 tablespoon lemon pepper seasoning

¼ cup grated Parmesan cheese

2 New York strip steaks

4 teaspoons salt

4 teaspoons ground black pepper

4 tablespoons butter

Pro tip: Always lay steaks away from you when placing them in the pan. The pan and oil are hot, and placing the steaks down toward you is a great way to get popped with piping-hot oil.

DIRECTIONS:

1. Preheat the oven to 375°F. Line a baking sheet with parchment or foil, if desired, for easy cleanup.
2. Spread the potatoes on the baking sheet.
3. Drizzle 2 tablespoons of the oil on the potatoes and sprinkle with 1 tablespoon each of the salt and lemon pepper seasoning.
4. Cook for 15 minutes and remove from the oven. Sprinkle with the Parmesan and cook for an additional 5 minutes.
5. While the potatoes are cooking, heat an empty cast-iron skillet on the stove over high heat.
6. Roll the steaks until each steak is no more than 1 inch thick.
7. Season each side of each steak with 1 teaspoon each of the salt and black pepper.
8. Drizzle the remaining 2 tablespoons of the oil into the hot pan and place the steaks in, laying them away from you. The steaks should sizzle vigorously when first touching the pan.
9. Cook for 3 minutes and then flip. Add the butter and, using a spoon, baste the tops of the steaks for about 4 minutes.
10. Remove from the pan and let rest for 8–10 minutes before serving with the potatoes.

FILET MIGNON OVER GRILLED PORTOBELLO WITH GARLIC-LEMON CREAM SAUCE

Sometimes, I like to spend a little extra on my grocery store budget. It all depends on my mood. The week I made this recipe, I was celebrating life. I was reunited with my husband after five long months (he joined the military), and I know how much Lew loves steak. I thought this would wow him, and it did. The filet was tender and juicy. The mushroom cap added an earthy aroma but maintained a level of sophistication, and the sauce tied everything together so harmoniously. Use this recipe for your next special occasion. (Yes, making it to Wednesday warrants a special occasion.)

PREP TIME: 5 MINUTES ❤ **COOK TIME:** 30 MINUTES ❤ **SERVES:** 2

INGREDIENTS:

SAUCE:

1 teaspoon minced garlic

2 tablespoons butter

1 cup heavy cream

1 teaspoon lemon juice or lemon zest

1 teaspoon finely chopped chives

1 teaspoon grated Parmesan cheese

Salt, to taste

Ground black pepper, to taste

FILET MIGNON:

4 teaspoons salt

4 teaspoons ground black pepper

2 filet mignon steaks

1 tablespoon grapeseed oil (or olive oil)

2 tablespoons butter

2 portobello mushroom caps

DIRECTIONS:

FOR THE SAUCE:

1. Place the garlic and the butter in a saucepan over medium-low heat.
2. Once the butter is bubbling and foamy, add the cream, lemon juice, and chives.
3. Cook for 10–15 minutes, until the sauce has thickened. (While the sauce is thickening, start the steaks.)
4. Remove from the heat. Stir in the Parmesan and salt and pepper to taste.

FOR THE FILET:

1. Preheat the oven to 350°F.
2. Season each steak on each side with 1 teaspoon each of the salt and pepper.
3. Heat a cast-iron skillet or other oven-safe pan until it is smoking hot, about 2–3 minutes over high heat.
4. Drizzle in the oil and add the steaks, laying them down away from you.
5. Sear for 2 minutes, or until that side of the steak is brown and crisp. There should be an almost glossy-looking finish on that side of the steak where the fats have started to caramelize.
6. Using a pair of tongs, hold one steak on its edge and sear for 1 minute. Repeat on the other edge, then place the steak on its cooked side once more, and sear both edges of the second steak.

Recipe Continues

7. Flip both steaks to sear the uncooked side. Add the butter and spoon over the tops of both steaks. Continue cooking and basting for 2 minutes.

8. Remove from the stove and place in the oven for 4 minutes, or until an inserted thermometer reads 130°F.

9. Carefully remove the pan from the oven and transfer to a clean board or plate.

10. Remove the stems from the portobello caps and place them ribbed side down in the same pan used to cook the steaks.

11. Cook on low heat for 4 minutes, then flip and cook the other side for an additional 4 minutes.

12. Remove from the heat. Place each portobello cap top side down on a plate and top with a filet.

13. Pour the sauce over the filet and enjoy.

Pro tip: You can tie these steaks with twine to preserve their shape and help cook them evenly.

CHAPTER TWELVE

MAMMA MIA, THAT'S A LOTTA PASTA!

Everyone has a tiny voice in their head. Sometimes it stops you from eating a tub of ice cream, sometimes it convinces you to get up and run in the morning. That voice whispers to me, "Pack up your bags and move to Italy, girl." I sometimes imagine myself in a gorgeous polka-dot, mid-calf dress. My hair is blowing freely in the wind. My high heels are not killing my feet with each step. My red lipstick is staying in place even though I've been eating pasta all day. (Shout out to Rihanna for the dope lip stain.) That hasn't happened to me yet, but I'm working on a little cookbook that I hope will give me the means to plan my dream Italy vacay one day. Until that happens, I'll settle for the things in everyday life that sing "Italy" to me. Yeah, let's make some pasta.

THE ART OF PASTA

I don't know if you've ever watched someone handcraft pasta, but it is truly an art form. There's something so intimate about working the dough with your hands. Also, on a less fantastical note, it's really freaking easy to make. Oh, you don't believe me? Come, I'll show you. This pasta recipe needs two ingredients and can be done without a pasta maker (that's right!). Throw your excuses to the side and welcome the world of fresh pasta into your heart.

HOW TO MAKE YOUR OWN PASTA FROM SCRATCH (IT'S EASY. PROMISE!)

PREP TIME: 1 HOUR, 45 MINUTES (DON'T LET THAT THROW YOU! MOST OF THAT IS CHILL TIME.)

COOK TIME: 4–6 MINUTES ❤ **SERVES:** 4–6

INGREDIENTS:

4 cups flour
4 eggs

DIRECTIONS:

1. Place 3 cups of the flour on a clean surface and shape it into a circle. (There should be prominent sides and a sunken center, forming a little volcano or well).

2. Crack the eggs into the well and, using a fork or spoon, gently beat the eggs into the surrounding flour.

3. Once most of the egg has been mixed with the flour and is no longer runny, use your hands and knuckles to knead the dough until it is yellow, elastic, and smooth.

4. Form the dough into a ball, cover in plastic wrap, and place in the fridge for 30 minutes or up to 4 hours.

5. Sprinkle a clean surface with ½ cup of the flour and roll out the chilled dough into a rectangle about ¼ to ⅛ inch thick.

6. Dust the top of dough with a little of the remaining flour and fold one short end two-thirds of the way in and fold the other short end on top of that, sprinkling flour in between each layer.

7. Make cuts widthwise across of the folded dough and cook in boiling water for 3–5 minutes.

8. Drain and serve immediately.

Pro tip: Try adding fresh ground herbs, lemon juice, or pureed veggies, like beets and corn, to pasta dough.

TUSCAN SALMON AND SPINACH MANICOTTI

My mom makes a salmon and shrimp keto meal that is just divine! However, I'm making pasta because, sometimes, carbs. This recipe is a beautiful symphony of the keto meal my mom loves and the pasta I crave. Like most great meals, the leftovers taste even better the next day. My husband is really into investing, which makes me think of this recipe: You spend a little money, put in a little work, wait a little bit, and reap a big reward. In our case, you spend a little money (and seriously only a little, 'cause budget-friendly cookbook!), you put in a little work (It truly is only a little work; whoever wrote this book really had the reader in mind. You're welcome!), wait a little bit (let them leftovers sit, baby), and reap a big reward. Huge understatement here: I love free food. If I can spend on a meal to feed me twice what I would spend on a meal to feed me once *and* it's better the next day? No brainer.

PREP TIME: 10 MINUTES ❤ **COOK TIME:** 45 MINUTES ❤ **SERVES:** 4–6

INGREDIENTS:

3 quarts water

8 ounces manicotti noodles

1 tablespoon salt

1½ pounds salmon

1 tablespoon Old Bay seasoning

2 tablespoons olive oil

2 tablespoons butter

2 tablespoons flour

1½ cups cherry tomatoes

½ cup chopped red onion

2 teaspoons minced garlic

4 cups heavy cream

2 cups spinach

½ cup grated Parmesan cheese

2 cups shredded mozzarella cheese

DIRECTIONS:

1. Bring the water to a boil. Add manicotti and salt. Cook until al dente, about 10 minutes. Leave the noodles in the water and set aside.
2. Season the salmon with the Old Bay seasoning.
3. Heat a skillet over high heat, then drizzle with the oil. Place the salmon skin side down in the pan. Cook over medium-high heat for 10 minutes, then flip, cooking the other side over low heat for 5 minutes. Remove from the heat and set aside.
4. In a saucepan, melt the butter over low heat until it begins to foam. Add the flour and stir until combined and clumpy.
5. Cook for 2 minutes, or until the mixture starts to thin, stirring continuously.
6. Add the tomatoes, onions, and garlic and cook over medium-high heat for 5 minutes, or until the tomatoes start to break down and the onions are soft.
7. Add the cream and simmer for 10 minutes.
8. Preheat the oven to 350°F.
9. Add the spinach and cover for 2 minutes, or until it begins to wilt.

Recipe Continues

10. Separate the salmon from its skin and flake (gently shred the flesh with a fork) it into the sauce. Add the Parmesan and stir well to combine.
11. Fill the manicotti with the salmon and place on a sheet pan.
12. Spread the remaining filling over the bottom of a 9 x 13-inch baking dish.
13. Move the manicotti from the sheet pan to the dish and top with the mozzarella.
14. Bake in the oven for 10 minutes, or until the cheese has melted and is slightly browned.
15. Remove from the oven and let rest a few minutes before serving.

Pro tip: Wait 5 minutes for the salmon filling to cool and place it in a piping bag. Cut off the tip and squeeze the filling into the manicotti noodles for a stress-free and mess-free experience.

SAUSAGE AND PEAS PENNE IN TOMATO CREAM SAUCE

Date night is not something you get often with three children and trust issues. (The list of people I let watch my children is shorter than the name of this dish.) Still, we do get out, maybe once every other year. This recipe is my copycat of the pasta dish I ordered on one of those glorious nights away. I don't remember the name of the restaurant, but I loved their pasta dish! It's quick and delicious. It'll feed your whole family, as long as you're not someone who falls subject to midnight cravings, like yours truly.

NO PREP TIME NEEDED (YOU'RE WELCOME) ♥ **COOK TIME:** 30 MINUTES ♥ **SERVES:** 6–8

INGREDIENTS:

12 ounces frozen peas (about 2 cups)

1 tablespoon olive oil

2 teaspoons minced garlic

2 cups grape medley tomatoes

3 quarts water

2 tablespoons salt

2½ cups heavy cream

10 basil leaves, chiffonade

1 teaspoon herbes de Provence

3–4 teaspoons Creole seasoning*

16 ounces penne noodles

1 pound Italian sausage

1 cup Parmesan cheese

* **Note:** I like to use Tony Chachere's Creole Seasoning.

> **Budget tip:** Grape tomatoes can be a little pricey. I sometimes use a can of diced tomatoes and green chiles in a pinch. If you opt for this ingredient instead, you can skip the wait time for the tomatoes to break down and form a sauce.

DIRECTIONS:

1. Cook the peas according to the package instructions and set aside.

2. Drizzle the oil into a pot over medium-low heat and add the garlic. Cook until the garlic begins to sizzle and becomes fragrant, about 2 minutes.

3. Add the tomatoes, squishing each with a slotted spoon to help break them down. Cook over medium-low heat for 4 minutes.

4. Meanwhile, pour the water and salt into a large pot over high heat for the penne.

5. Add the cream, basil, herbes de Provence, and Creole seasoning to the tomato sauce.

6. Cook until the sauce begins to thicken and tomatoes have completely broken down, about 20 minutes. The sauce will bubble and become light red in color.

7. When the pasta water is boiling, add the penne and cook for about 15 minutes, until the noodles are soft and chewy.

8. While the sauce and penne are cooking, remove the sausage from the casings and place in a skillet over medium-high heat. (I like to use a cast-iron skillet, but any nonstick skillet will do just fine.) Crush meat to preferred fineness and brown, about 15 minutes.

Recipe Continues

9. Drain the penne and remove the sauce and sausage from the heat when done.

10. Combine the penne and sauce in a large pan or bowl. Mix in the peas, sausage, and Parmesan. Bring the whole bowl over to the kitchen table and let the hungry bellies dig in. Sit back and enjoy a night brought together by your hands. Sure, it's my recipe, but it was you who put it all together!

Pro tip: My kids are picky eaters, so we put half of the noodles to the side and serve them plain with a side of peas and a little bit of sausage before combining.

CREOLE MAC AND CHEESE

In my opinion, this might be my craziest recipe in this book. Call it a product tester. Make this macaroni dish and then let me know if I should break out the archives of all the wacky food combos that live in my head. Classics are reliable. Zany creations are fun and new. I think every foodie needs a good balance of both. This recipe is my combination of a Louisiana-style pasta and the creamy goodness of macaroni and cheese. I could eat this every day for at least two weeks before I'd need to switch things up. Try it tonight if you're feeling a little spicy! And if you just so happen to eat the leftovers for breakfast, lunch, and dinner the next day, I won't judge you. Not one bit . . . nope, not one bit.

PREP TIME: 10 MINUTES ❤ **COOK TIME:** 40 MINUTES ❤ **SERVES:** 4-6

INGREDIENTS:

3 quarts water

16 ounces (2 cups) elbow macaroni

1 chicken bouillon cube

1 tablespoon salt

1 tablespoon olive oil

1 red bell pepper, thinly sliced

1 yellow bell pepper, thinly sliced

6–7 ounces andouille sausage

1/2 pound sliced chicken breast

6 ounces raw shrimp, deveined and tails removed

1 tablespoon Creole seasoning*

1 teaspoon cayenne pepper

1 teaspoon red pepper flakes

1 stick (1/2 cup) butter

1/2 cup flour

3 cups whole milk or heavy cream

1 cup grated cheddar cheese

1 cup grated pepper Jack cheese

1/4 cup chopped chives (for garnish)

* **Note:** I like to use Tony Chachere's Creole Seasoning.

> **Budget tip:** Have leftovers? Don't just store them. Scoop leftovers into bite-sized balls and freeze overnight. Dredge in beaten egg and then flour before transferring to a pan of canola oil for fried mac and cheese balls!

DIRECTIONS:

1. In a large pot, bring the water to a rapid boil. Add the macaroni, bouillon cube, and salt and simmer for 15–20 minutes, to your desired doneness. Drain and set aside.
2. Meanwhile, heat a skillet over high heat and drizzle in the oil. When the oil starts to look runny, add the peppers and cook for 3 minutes.
3. Halve the sausage and cut into 1/2-inch slices. Add the sausage, flat-side down, and brown for 3 minutes.
4. Add the chicken and cook for 4 minutes.
5. Add the shrimp, Creole seasoning, cayenne, and red pepper flakes and cook for 3–4 minutes, until the shrimp is pink and slightly curled.
6. In a separate pot, melt the butter over medium-high heat.
7. Sprinkle in the flour and whisk until combined. Continue whisking and cooking until the mix thins out, 3–5 minutes.
8. Add the milk and simmer for 15–20 minutes, until thickened enough to coat the back of a spoon.
9. Add the cheeses and remove from the heat, stirring until the cheese has melted and is completely combined.
10. Combine the macaroni, meat and veggie mixture, and cheese sauce. Garnish with the chives and serve warm.

FETTUCCINE ALFREDO

I tried a store-bought Alfredo sauce once. I learned my lesson and made this recipe immediately after. Some people like the store-bought Alfredo sauce, but I just could not get through a bottle of it. Even on my laziest nights, I still muster up the energy to make this sauce over the canned stuff. I don't think I've given out any assignments in this book, so here is the first: Make the doggone Alfredo sauce, sis.

PREP TIME: 5 MINUTES ♥ **COOK TIME:** 20 MINUTES ♥ **SERVES:** 5–6

INGREDIENTS:

2 quarts water

1 tablespoon plus 1 teaspoon salt

16 ounces fettuccine

1 stick (½ cup) butter

1 tablespoon minced garlic

2 cups (16 ounces) heavy cream

8-ounce package cream cheese

1 teaspoon ground black pepper

1 teaspoon garlic powder

1 teaspoon onion powder

2 teaspoons freeze-dried chives

Pro tip: This is a perfect recipe to try with the Pasta from Scratch recipe on page 160.

DIRECTIONS:

1. In a large pot, bring the water and 1 tablespoon of the salt to a boil and add the fettuccine.

2. Reduce the heat to low and cook for 15–20 minutes, until soft and easily bendable (al dente). Drain and set aside.

3. Meanwhile, in a medium saucepan, melt the butter and cook the garlic for 1–2 minutes, until the garlic is fragrant and golden brown.

4. Pour in the cream and simmer for 10–12 minutes, until thick enough to coat the back of a spoon.

5. Cut the cream cheese into fourths so it's easier to melt and add them to the pot of cream.

6. Stir for 3–5 minutes, until the cheese is completely melted.

7. Remove from the heat and add the remaining 1 teaspoon salt as well as the pepper, garlic powder, onion powder, and chives.

8. Pour over the fettuccine and enjoy.

LASAGNA ROLL-UPS

Lasagna is my husband's favorite meal. So, I knew I had to perfect this classic dish soon after we met. Some people flaunt their money, some pretend to love sports, I saw some guys join the drama club just to win over their crush.... Your girl, however, learned how to make a bomb lasagna. Now here we are, seven years later, married with three kids, so you better believe that lasagna is magic. Still, the best lasagna I've ever tasted came from the graciousness of my pastor's wife. After I had my third child, she brought some for my family. I admit, my family had far less of it than I did (no regrets at all!). I never got her recipe, but I imagine it tasted so amazing because it was filled with love. I savored every bite, sniffed, took notes, and created a recipe that I get asked to make all the time. Here's my rendition of her masterpiece, also filled with love, and a bunch of other really tasty stuff!

PREP TIME: 10 MINUTES ♥ **COOK TIME:** 1 HOUR ♥ **SERVES:** 6–8

INGREDIENTS:

NOODLES:
3 quarts water

1 teaspoon salt

1 package lasagna noodles

FILLING:
1 tablespoon olive oil

2 green peppers, diced

1 red pepper, diced

½ medium white onion, diced

½ medium red onion, diced

1 pound pork sausage

SAUCE:
2 tablespoons olive oil

2 tablespoons minced garlic

28-ounce can whole tomatoes

½ cup basil leaves, chiffonade

3 tablespoons granulated sugar

1 tablespoon salt

1 tablespoon ground black pepper

1 tablespoon Italian seasoning

¼ cup grated Parmesan cheese

SECRET WEAPON:
16 ounces ricotta cheese

4 ounces cream cheese

1 cup spinach, packed

1 egg

1 teaspoon garlic powder

1 teaspoon onion powder

1 teaspoon freeze-dried chives

½ teaspoon paprika

1 tablespoon sun-dried tomatoes

TOPPING:
3 cups shredded Italian blend cheese

DIRECTIONS:

1. Preheat the oven to 350°F.

FOR THE NOODLES:

1. Bring the water and salt to a boil in a large pot over high heat.
2. Add the noodles and simmer for 10–15 minutes, until al dente.
3. Remove from the heat and drain.
4. Place in a bowl of cold water until ready to use.

Recipe Continues

FOR THE FILLING:

1. Drizzle the oil in a skillet over medium-high heat Add the peppers and onions and cook for about 5 minutes, until the peppers are somewhat soft and the onions start to look translucent.
2. Add the sausage and, using a rubber spatula or wooden spoon, grind it into small pieces. Cook until the sausage is browned, about 5 minutes.
3. Remove from the heat and set aside.

FOR THE SAUCE:

1. Heat the oil in a medium saucepan over medium-low heat until it can easily spread around the bottom of the pan.
2. Add the garlic and cook for about 2 minutes, stirring often to make sure it doesn't burn.
3. Dump the entire contents of the tomato can into the pan along with the basil, sugar, salt, pepper, and Italian seasoning.
4. Cook for 10 minutes, or until the tomatoes have broken down into a liquid. (If you want a thinner sauce, you can blend the mixture in a blender or by using an immersion blender.)
5. Once the sauce is at your desired consistency, remove from the heat and fold in the Parmesan.

FOR THE SECRET WEAPON AND ASSEMBLY:

1. Put all ingredients for the secret filling into a blender and blend for about 30 seconds to 1 minute, until smooth and a bright, pea-like green color.
2. To assemble, pour sauce in the bottom of a 9 x 13-inch baking pan.
3. On a clean working surface, lay out four or five noodles.
4. Spread a spoonful of the secret weapon along the length of each noodle, then spread a spoonful of the meat filling on top of it, also along the length of the noodle.
5. Carefully roll each noodle, enclosing the fillings until the entire noodle has been rolled.
6. Transfer to the baking pan directly on top of the sauce.
7. Repeat with the remaining lasagna noodles.
8. Sprinkle with the topping, the Italian blend cheese.
9. Bake in the oven for 30 minutes, or until the cheese is bubbling and slightly browned. Let rest for a few minutes before serving.

> **Pro tip:** Want a more traditional lasagna? Ditch rolling the noodles and place a layer flat inside a baking pan with enough of the sauce to cover the bottom. Layer your pasta by adding layers of the secret weapon, meat, and sauce. Top with another row of noodles and repeat the layers until you've reached the top of the pan. Cover with cheese and bake for 30 minutes, or until the cheese has browned.

CHAPTER THIRTEEN

WORTHY, FLIRTY, AND READY IN 30

(30-MINUTE-PREP MEALS)

This chapter might be my favorite. Before kids, I could spend hours prepping, cooking, and beautifully plating a meal. Three kids and one husband later, if a recipe is going to take me longer than an hour, I'm probably not making it. That's why this section is so close to my heart. Whatever your personal circumstances, there are going to be those days when time is not on your side. Put down the phone because these recipes will be ready to eat before your food delivery order arrives. Go ahead, flirt with time a little.

RUSTIC PIZZA PUFFS

There are two foods that take me back to my college days: ramen noodles and pizza rolls. This recipe is all about embracing the nostalgia of those late-night study sessions. I'm elevating these pizza rolls, of course, because we're grown now. There are very few ingredients involved in this dish, which makes it the perfect go-to recipe for the nights when you could use a bit of quick comfort food. This recipe takes about as long to make as it does to eat.

PREP TIME: 15 MINUTES ❤ **COOK TIME:** 5 MINUTES PER BATCH ❤ **SERVES:** 6

INGREDIENTS:

5 cups canola oil

2 tablespoons olive oil

2 tablespoons minced garlic

28-ounce can whole tomatoes

½ cup basil leaves, chiffonade

2 tablespoons granulated sugar

1 tablespoon salt

1 tablespoon ground black pepper

1 tablespoon Italian seasoning

1 pound ground beef

2 cans refrigerated pizza dough, such as Pillsbury Pizza Crust

16 ounces shredded mozzarella cheese

6 ounces pepperoni slices

Pro tip: Try cooking these in the air fryer or oven for 13–15 minutes at 350°F for an easier, healthier option.

DIRECTIONS:

1. Heat the canola oil in a large pot over medium-high heat.
2. Meanwhile, heat the olive oil in a small saucepan over medium-low heat for 20 seconds, or until hot enough to easily run along the bottom of the pan. Add the garlic and cook until fragrant, about 1–2 minutes, stirring often so it doesn't burn.
3. Add the tomatoes, basil, sugar, salt, pepper, and the Italian seasoning to the saucepan. Cook until the tomatoes start to break down and form a chunky sauce, 8–10 minutes. Remove from the heat.
4. Brown the beef in a skillet over medium-high heat until cooked through. Remove from the heat.
5. On a lightly floured surface, unroll the pizza dough and make line impressions with a pizza cutter, forming 6 equal rectangles. (Make 1 line that runs lengthwise through the middle of the dough, and two lines equally spaced widthwise.)
6. On the top three rectangles, make layers of cheese, sauce, meat, pepperoni, and more cheese.
7. Fold the bottom three rectangles up and over the top three. Cut along the two lines to separate the three pockets.
8. Using a fork or your fingers, firmly press down the edges of each pizza pocket to secure the sides of the dough and stop any filling from escaping.
9. Gently place the pockets in the hot pot of canola oil and cook for 2 minutes on each side, using tongs to flip them over. The crust should be golden brown.
10. Let rest a few minutes before serving.

SMOTHERED PORK CHOPS AND RICE

Any smothered food is enough to make me leap for joy. This pork chop recipe is a prime example of smothered-food = joy. After getting a nice golden crust on the pork chops, I use the same pan to create a gravy that is out of this world! We like to eat this with a side of rice. It's cheap and easy, and the rice can cook without much attention while you focus your energy on the real star of the meal: the pork chops. I love recipes with components that are super hands off. Some days my brain isn't as sharp as on other days, and I can't multitask enough to make a complex dish. This recipe is perfect for those hectic days, without compromising on flavor.

PREP TIME: 2 MINUTES ♥ **COOK TIME:** 25 MINUTES ♥ **SERVES:** 3–5

INGREDIENTS:

2 cups rice

4 cups plus 1 teaspoon water

5 tablespoons butter

2 pounds thin pork chops

1 tablespoon salt

1 tablespoon ground black pepper

1 tablespoon grapeseed oil or other oil with a high smoke point

16 ounces sliced baby bella mushrooms

1 medium white onion, thinly sliced

½ teaspoon cornstarch

2 cups heavy cream

1 teaspoon freeze-dried chives

½ teaspoon paprika

½ teaspoon cayenne pepper

DIRECTIONS:

1. Bring the rice and 4 cups water to a rolling boil in a saucepan over high heat.
2. Add 2 tablespoons of the butter. Cover, reduce the heat to low, and cook for 20 minutes, until the water has been absorbed.
3. Meanwhile, season each pork chop with about ¼ teaspoon each of the salt and pepper.
4. Heat a large cast-iron skillet over high heat until smoking hot, about 3 minutes.
5. Drizzle in the oil and carefully add the pork in one layer, working in batches.
6. Cook for 1 minute and flip. Add 1½ tablespoons of the butter and cook for 1 minute.
7. Transfer to a plate lined with paper towels and continue cooking the remaining pork chops (you do not need to add more butter with subsequent batches).
8. Cook the mushrooms and onions in the same skillet over medium-high heat for about 2 minutes, coating the veggies in the leftover pork bits.
9. Make a slurry by combining the cornstarch and 1 teaspoon water. Pour into the skillet.
10. Add the cream, chives, paprika, cayenne, and the remaining 1½ tablespoons butter.
11. Cook for 15 minutes, or until the sauce is slightly thick and a light brown color.
12. Add pork chops to the sauce and let simmer for 2 minutes.
13. Serve with the rice.

Pro tip: If you have the money to buy thick-cut pork chops, increase your cook time to 4 minutes on one side over medium-high heat. Then turn the heat to high and cook the other side until browned, about 2 minutes.

CABBAGE STEAKS

This recipe was inspired by my beautiful mother. I never would've thought to cook cabbage this way. After she taught me how to make them, I knew they needed to make an appearance in this book. Sometimes I want a light meal, something super easy to just pop in the oven and enjoy. For a heartier meal, pair these steaks with baked chicken. Check the "Dinner's Ready!" section on page 133 for chicken cooking tips and tricks.

PREP TIME: 5 MINUTES ❤ **COOK TIME:** 25 MINUTES ❤ **SERVES:** 3–5

INGREDIENTS:

1 large head cabbage

3 tablespoons olive oil

1 tablespoon salt

1 tablespoon lemon pepper seasoning

6 teaspoons grated Parmesan cheese

½ ounce sliced salami

1 cup (8 ounces) marinara sauce

4 ounces sliced mozzarella cheese

Budget tip: Looking to stretch this meal even further? These cabbage steaks are great with roasted zucchini and yellow squash. Wash and dice veggies and spread on a baking sheet. Drizzle with 1 tablespoon olive oil and 1 teaspoon each of salt and pepper. Put them in the oven with the cabbage steaks and also cook for 20–25 minutes.

DIRECTIONS:

1. Preheat the oven to 375°F.
2. Thoroughly wash the cabbage and slice into ¼-inch rounds. You should be able to cut about six cabbage steaks.
3. Lay the cabbage steaks flat on a baking sheet and drizzle with the oil.
4. Season each steak with ½ teaspoon salt, ½ teaspoon lemon pepper seasoning, and 1 teaspoon Parmesan.
5. Fold each salami slice in half and place sporadically within the folds of the cabbage steaks.
6. Top each with the marinara sauce and mozzarella.
7. Cook for 20–25 minutes, until the cheese is melted and bubbling and the cabbage is al dente.

FRIED CAULIFLOWER RICE

My kids are not the only picky eaters in the family. Sometimes both Lewis and I need a little extra persuasion to eat our veggies. This meal makes that mission incredibly easy! I honestly don't even miss actual rice when eating this. Did I mention the whole thing comes together in less than 30 minutes? Veggies, check. Delicious, check. One of the easiest meals you'll ever make? You guessed it, check!

PREP TIME: 10 MINUTES ♥ **COOK TIME:** 15 MINUTES ♥ **SERVES:** 3–6

INGREDIENTS:

1 large head cauliflower

2 tablespoons canola oil

12-ounce package frozen vegetable medley

2 teaspoons minced garlic

1 teaspoon grated ginger

¼ cup soy sauce

1 cup bean sprouts

2 eggs, beaten

1 tablespoon sesame oil

Pro tip: For a heartier option, add sautéed shrimp and/or chicken.

DIRECTIONS:

1. To grate the cauliflower, remove leaves from the base. Hold by the stem over a baking sheet or other pan, to catch the grated pieces. With your other hand, grate the cauliflower in its entirety, leaving only the thick stem.

2. Heat the canola oil in a large skillet over medium-high heat and add the cauliflower. Cook for 5 minutes, using a rubber spatula to gently stir the cauliflower after each minute.

3. Microwave the vegetable medley for 4 minutes.

4. Add the veggies, garlic, ginger, and soy sauce to the cauliflower. Cook for 3 minutes.

5. Stir in the bean sprouts.

6. Create a well in the middle of the cauliflower mixture, exposing the bottom of the skillet. Pour the beaten eggs into the well. Fold until the eggs are fully cooked, about 2 minutes.

7. Drizzle with the sesame oil and stir, incorporating both the sesame oil and eggs.

8. Serve immediately.

ONE-POT CHICKEN THIGHS

My husband does this adorable thing—occasionally he comes home for lunch. The kids love their midday daddy jungle gym time. What that means for me, though, is the added, self-imposed pressure to make something extraordinary for him. Lewis could care less if I gave him a bowl of boxed mac and cheese or a bologna sandwich, but I'm a bit of an overachiever. When he comes home, I gotta have some "get in my belly" smells filling our home. With only 20 minutes' notice that he's coming home for lunch, I need something to feed my people, fast! So, the one-pot-of-chicken-thighs dish was born. I abracadabra(d) the mess out of some veggies and chicken, threw it all in a pot, and acted like it had been cooking the whole time. He is none the wiser (unless he reads this, so until then, no one tell him!). While this recipe was originally for Lewis's lunch breaks, it has since become a dinner staple in my house. At this stage in my life, it's rare if I'm not scrambling over here, trying to run a house full of people who are set on destroying it and testing every last string of my patience. Meals like this are a necessity. Just throw everything in the pot, forget about it for 20 minutes, and—boom—it's done.

PREP TIME: 10 MINUTES ❤ **COOK TIME:** 30 MINUTES ❤ **SERVES:** 3–6

INGREDIENTS:

3 tablespoons butter

2 teaspoons minced garlic

1 medium red onion, sliced

1 medium yellow onion, sliced

1 red pepper, sliced

1 yellow pepper, sliced

1 green pepper, sliced

3 potatoes, cubed

1 cup chicken broth

1½–2 pounds boneless chicken thighs

3 teaspoons Creole seasoning*

1 teaspoon Italian seasoning

* **Note:** I like to use Tony Chachere's Creole Seasoning.

DIRECTIONS:

1. Melt the butter in a skillet over medium heat. Add the garlic and stir for 30 seconds.

2. Add the onions, peppers, potatoes, and ½ cup of the chicken broth.

3. Cover and cook for 15 minutes, briefly stirring every 5 minutes.

4. Season the chicken with the Creole seasoning, massaging it in. It should look seasoned but shouldn't be completely covered. (Add more seasoning if needed.)

5. With a rubber spatula or spoon, move the veggies around in the skillet to create small spaces for the chicken to touch the bottom of the pan.

6. Add the chicken and spread the veggies on top. Add the remaining ½ cup chicken broth and sprinkle the Italian seasoning on top.

7. Cover and cook for 10–15 minutes, until the chicken is cooked through* and the flesh is brownish-pink but not bright pink. The onions and peppers should be soft, and the potatoes should slip off the end of a knife when punctured.

Recipe Continues

8. Serve by the spoonful, grabbing a piece of chicken and as much vegetable mixture as your heart desires.

* **Note:** Test the doneness of the chicken by making a small incision in one of the thickest pieces, turn the knife sideways, and check to make sure the chicken is white inside and the juices are clear (not pink).

Budget tip: Want to make this meal go even further? Add an extra cup of chicken broth. Then, in a medium saucepan, bring 4 cups water and 2 cups rice to a rolling boil. Once the rice starts to boil, reduce the heat to low and cover. Cook over low heat for 15–20 minutes, until the water has been absorbed and the rice is tender (refer to the "Rice Ratios" section on page 11) . Fluff with a fork and serve under a heaping scoop of chicken and veggies. The extra broth added to the recipe will serve as a nice sauce for the rice.

The Cherry on Top!

We could've ended this book with dinner, but what's the fun in that? My kids are constantly asking for treats after meals. "Mom, I ate all my food. Can I *please* have a treat now?" Some days I say no, but most days, they get an enthusiastic yes! So let's all give a big collective excited yes to keep the party going just a little longer with a chapter of desserts sure to put the cherry on top of any day.

CHAPTER FOURTEEN

DELIGHTFUL DESSERTS

I learned to remember to spell dessert by memorizing how to spell desert, adding an "s" because you always want more of it. The recipes in this chapter will definitely leave you wanting more. Some might say I have a stronger-than-average sweet tooth. (Some might be right too.) Whether you crave something sweet every day or once a month, these recipes are crave-worthy. Even better, you'll spend the same amount of money on a whole batch as you would for one serving of these desserts in a restaurant. Tasty treats are almost always cheapest to make at home. Nothing is as inexpensive, yet as priceless, as a little flour, a cup of sugar, and oodles of love.

PEANUT BUTTER AND CHOCOLATE COOKIES

I've adored peanut butter and chocolate since I was ten years old. Once, I accidentally made a peanut butter and chocolate cookie in my microwave. Don't worry: These cookies are much better, anything but accidental. I had to get some help from my mentor, Cristina Curp from the Castaway Kitchen, for this recipe. She is a genius and was such a rock for me throughout this whole experience. She agreed that my vision of the perfectly harmonious peanut butter cookie needed to come to life. Graciously, what came out of my oven was pure heaven.

PREP TIME: 40 MINUTES ❤ **COOK TIME:** 10 MINUTES ❤ **YIELD:** 1 DOZEN

INGREDIENTS:

½ cup peanut butter

1 stick (½ cup) butter, softened

½ cup granulated sugar

½ cup brown sugar

1 teaspoon vanilla extract

1 egg

1¾ cups flour

1 teaspoon salt

¼ cup dark chocolate (chopped into chunks)

DIRECTIONS:

1. In a stand mixer or bowl, beat together the peanut butter and butter until smooth.
2. Add the sugars and mix until combined.
3. Mix in the vanilla and egg until completely incorporated. You should have a smooth base.
4. Add the flour and salt and combine until a dough forms.
5. Fold in the chocolate chunks.
6. Wrap in plastic wrap and refrigerate for 30 minutes to 1 hour.
7. Preheat the oven to 375°F.
8. Unwrap the chilled dough.
9. Using a spoon or scooper, scoop 1-inch balls of dough and place 2 inches apart on an ungreased baking sheet.
10. Using your fingers or the back of a fork, flatten each ball onto the baking sheet.
11. Bake in the oven for 8–10 minutes, until slightly browned.
12. Let cool on a wire rack or plate for 5 minutes and enjoy.

GRANDMA'S SUGAR COOKIES

These cookies bring delightful memories with them. My grandma on my mom's side has a bit of a sweet tooth (like yours truly) and has been making this recipe for me since forever. You can cover these cookies with sprinkles or icing or enjoy them plain. They're delicious all three ways. The moist, melt-in-your-mouth experience of biting into this perfect confection is something everyone should experience at least once.

PREP TIME: 10 MINUTES ♥ **COOK TIME:** 8 MINUTES PER BATCH ♥ **YIELD:** 2 DOZEN

INGREDIENTS:

3 cups flour

1¼ cups granulated sugar

1 teaspoon baking powder

1 teaspoon baking soda

½ teaspoon ground nutmeg (optional)

1 cup sour cream

½ cup vegetable shortening

1 stick (½ cup) butter, softened

2 eggs

1 teaspoon vanilla extract

¼ cup milk

> **Pro tip:** If you are rolling out the dough to make cookie-cutter-shaped cookies, my grandma recommends adding another 1½ to 2 cups flour.

DIRECTIONS:

1. Preheat the oven to 350°F.
2. In a medium bowl, combine the flour, 1 cup of the sugar, the baking powder, baking soda, and nutmeg.
3. In a separate bowl, whisk (or use a spoon to mix) together the sour cream, shortening, and butter until smooth, about 2 minutes.
4. Add the eggs, one at a time, and beat until combined, about 30 seconds after each egg. Be careful not to overwork the dough.
5. Stir in the vanilla.
6. Slowly combine the dry and wet ingredients until a soft dough forms.
7. Form into balls, about 1½ inches in diameter, and place 2 inches apart on an ungreased baking sheet.
8. Dip the top of a cloth in the milk, cover the balls, and press down on the cloth to gently flatten cookies.
9. Sprinkle each cookie with the remaining ¼ cup of sugar.
10. Bake for 7–10 minutes, until slightly golden and fluffy.
11. Let cool on a wire rack or plate for 5 minutes and enjoy.

TEA CAKES

When I was asked to help cater a Juneteenth celebration, I wanted to make foods that represented the culture and people. Strawberry soda pop symbolized the blood lost through the harsh realities of slavery. To complement that symbolic drink, I prepared hundreds of tea cakes. This is not a typical cake that you might find at a wedding. These cakes are shaped more like cookies, with crisp edges and chewy centers reminiscent of a snickerdoodle. These cakes date back through generations. Slaves were allotted very few ingredients, and with sparse quantities. Tea cakes were made with molasses, lard, eggs, and flour. Nowadays, we may consider these ingredients to be basic necessities, but they were luxuries then. This recipe captures the essence of those traditional cakes that brought so many people joy. I love these tea cakes because they're a true testament to the power of food to lift spirits and bring people together.

PREP TIME: 2 HOURS, 10 MINUTES ❤ **COOK TIME:** 8 MINUTES PER BATCH ❤ **YIELD:** 4 DOZEN

INGREDIENTS:

2 ½ cups flour

1 teaspoon cinnamon

¼ teaspoon salt

½ teaspoon baking soda

½ teaspoon nutmeg

2 sticks (1 cup) butter, softened

1 ½ cups granulated sugar

2 eggs

DIRECTIONS:

1. In a medium bowl, combine the flour, cinnamon, salt, baking soda, and nutmeg. Stir thoroughly, until fully combined.
2. Whip the butter in a separate medium bowl until pale yellow and smooth. (A stand or hand mixer is useful, but you can also hand-beat the butter with a whisk.)
3. Add the sugar and mix until combined.
4. Add the eggs and mix until fully incorporated.
5. Slowly pour in the dry ingredients and stir until everything is mixed and the dough is stiff and slightly tan.
6. Wrap tightly in plastic wrap and place in the fridge for at least 2 hours.
7. Preheat the oven to 350°F.
8. Unwrap the chilled dough.
9. Using a tablespoon, scoop sections of the dough into the palm of your hand and roll into small balls (about 1½ inches wide).
10. Using your middle and index fingers, press the center of each ball down, spreading the dough and leaving a ¼-inch perimeter slightly raised.
11. Place a batch of 12 cookies at a time on an ungreased baking sheet.
12. Bake in the oven for 8 minutes, or until the edges are golden brown.
13. Remove and place on a platter to eat immediately, because freedom took long enough.

ALL-THAT APPLE CRISP

I feel like Sam I Am from Dr. Seuss's *Green Eggs and Ham*, except with this apple crisp. I could eat it in a plane, sitting with that girl Jane. I could eat it at the movies, while feeling super groovy. Yes, to be fair, I could eat this apple crisp anywhere. I admit, I'm better at cooking than rhyming. Good thing I have this ridiculously easy apple crisp recipe to indulge me. Hear me scream as I enjoy with ice cream, and let no one be stopping that swirl of fresh whipped topping!

PREP TIME: 15 MINUTES ♥ **COOK TIME:** 45 MINUTES ♥ **SERVES:** 8–10

INGREDIENTS:

6 red apples, cored and thinly sliced

¼ cup granulated sugar

2 teaspoons ground cinnamon

¾ cup brown sugar

¾ cup rolled oats

¾ cup flour

1 stick (½ cup) butter, cubed

DIRECTIONS:

1. Preheat the oven to 350°F.
2. Toss the apple slices in a bowl with the granulated sugar and 1 teaspoon of the cinnamon.
3. Transfer to a 9-inch baking dish.
4. In a separate bowl, stir together the brown sugar, oats, flour, and the remaining teaspoon cinnamon until fully combined.
5. Use a fork or gloved fingers to work the butter into the oat mixture until the oats are crumbly and damp.
6. Spread the oat mixture over the apples.
7. Bake in the oven for 45–50 minutes, until the apples are tender and the crust crispy and slightly browned.
8. Remove from the oven, let cool slightly, and serve warm.

FLIP-ME-UPSIDE-DOWN PINEAPPLE CAKE

To me, cooking is like poetry. I love bringing ingredients together like the words of a poem. Once combined, they evoke emotions powerful enough to make people sit back and say, "*Wow.*" In this recipe, I present to you my kitchen poetry, in the form of a simple, spongy, tangy cake.

PREP TIME: 10 MINUTES ❤ **COOK TIME:** 15 MINUTES ❤ **YIELD:** 12 MINI CAKES

INGREDIENTS:

6 tablespoons butter, melted

15.25-ounce package yellow cake mix

1 cup pineapple juice

3 eggs

10 ounces crushed pineapple (about 2⅓ cups)

12 blackberries or maraschino cherries

DIRECTIONS:

1. Preheat the oven to 350°F.
2. Beat together the cake mix, butter, pineapple juice, and eggs until smooth and fluffy, about 3 minutes.
3. Place 1 tablespoon of the crushed pineapple into the bottom of each cup of a muffin pan. There should be enough pineapple to cover the bottom but not fill more than ½ inch of the cup's height.
4. Place one blackberry in the center of each muffin cup.
5. Top each with 2 spoonfuls of the batter.
6. Bake in the oven for 12–15 minutes, until the tops are browned and a knife dipped in the center comes out clean.
7. Allow to cool completely before flipping the pan upside down and removing each mini cake.
8. Enjoy these poetry slam-dunk cakes and throw out some snaps for me as you eat these with the ones who make your heart sing.

SHAKE-THAT-TAFFY APPLE SALAD

This gem is a simple recipe with simple ingredients and an outstanding flavor profile. It's a true "shake that taffy apple" kind of dessert salad. My mom used to make this apple salad for church picnics or any summertime event that needed a bit of refreshing deliciousness.

PREP TIME: 15 MINUTES ❤ **REST TIME:** 1 HOUR ❤ **SERVES:** 8–10

INGREDIENTS:

4 green apples, cored and chopped

4 full-size (1.86-ounce) Snickers bars, chopped

16 ounces (about 2 cups) whipped cream

3.4-ounce pouch instant vanilla pudding

DIRECTIONS:

1. Toss the apples and Snickers into a bowl.
2. Add the whipped cream and pudding mix.
3. Stir to combine.
4. Refrigerate for 1 hour.
5. Serve chilled.

BEST-EST, FUDGE-IEST, BROWNIE-EST BROWNIE

If you haven't guessed already, I love brownies far more than the average brownie lover. I will never turn down a brownie. I don't care what I'm doing. Topped with ice cream, filled with cookie dough, or plain, I've tried them every way imaginable, and I *love* them. This recipe right here, though! Straight chocolate-infused fudge fire. Skip the trip to the grocery store, forget the food delivery service, and head to your kitchen to make these any time your belly craves chocolate. This is a recipe that will satisfy even the biggest chocolate-craving sweet tooth. You might want to consider hiding a brownie before serving the rest; they will go fast, and I will say I told you so.

PREP TIME: 10 MINUTES ❤ **COOK TIME:** 20 MINUTES ❤ **SERVES:** 7–9

INGREDIENTS:

4 tablespoons butter, plus more for greasing

¼ cup vegetable shortening

1 cup granulated sugar

2 eggs

1 teaspoon vanilla extract

½ cup flour

⅓ cup unsweetened cocoa powder

¼ cup semisweet chocolate chips

DIRECTIONS:

1. Preheat the oven to 350°F. Grease an 8-inch baking pan with some butter.
2. Melt the butter and shortening in a small saucepan over medium heat. Remove from the heat.
3. Add the sugar and mix until light and smooth.
4. Beat the eggs and vanilla in a separate bowl.
5. While whisking vigorously, slowly incorporate the sugar mixture into the eggs and vanilla.
6. Add the flour and cocoa. Mix for about 2 minutes, until fully combined.
7. Incorporate the chocolate chips.
8. Spread in the prepared baking pan.
9. Bake in the oven for 20 minutes, or until a knife dipped in the center comes out clean, with a few crumbles.
10. Let sit in the pan for 15 minutes before cutting and serving.

ACKNOWLEDGMENTS

FIRST THANKS AND CREDIT GO to God, who orchestrates and blesses my life. I am so incredibly grateful.

I want to acknowledge my husband, Lewis: You have been a rock for me throughout my entire culinary career. You have kept me sane with your offerings, actions as small as doing the dishes to as big as relieving me from parental duties. I love you with all my heart.

To Luke, Lena, and Luna: It's an honor to be your mama and watch you grow. It brings me so much joy to see you all taking an interest in the kitchen. It's that interest that keeps me cooking on the days when I'm most exhausted.

To my parents and bonus parents: Thank you for the countless encouraging phone calls and for taking on the titles of grandparent *and* babysitter. Through the months when Lew was in training, and I was left alone with the kids, you were such tremendous support. That support gave me the extra courage to write this book and chase my dreams.

To Mama Anne and my late grandfather Papa Fred: You were both so instrumental to my childhood. You made me feel loved, welcomed, and included. You opened up your home and kitchen and poured love into my life through your faith and food. I am forever grateful.

To my sweet Auntie Lovie, whom everyone does indeed love: I have always looked up to you. Your culinary career inspired me to venture into my own. I wouldn't be here writing this book if it weren't for your influence, passion, and expertise. Thank you. I love you so much.

To my family, my grandparents, my aunts, uncles, and cousins, both through blood and through choice: Your network of support has given me a soft place to land through all my mistakes and successes, a place I often go to when I feel extra self-critical.

To Gordon and the *MasterChef* team: Thank you for picking me from among the masses, pouring into me, believing in me, and pushing me to grow. I am forever grateful for the blessing of that experience, which continues to mold and encourage me even now, years later.

To the wonderful *MasterChef* cast: I feel bonded to all fifteen of you for life. You have become my family.

To my best friend, Makaehla Harrington: Never before have I had a friend so consistently by my side. A friend who I run to with all my failures and all of my accomplishments. A friend who encourages, loves, checks in on, and uplifts me as you do. Throughout this process, you have been most supportive. You have sent me gift cards, prayers, encouraging letters, and even helped me brainstorm title suggestions. To my friend-turned-family, thank you.

To my dear friend Maryann: You pushed me to start this journey. To try out for *MasterChef,* continue to cook, and even partner with you and teach. You are always there for me when I need it most, and I am so grateful to have you in my life.

To Joelle and Christian Price, my newest friends and favorite "kick it" couple: You have done more for me in the few months we've known each other than most past friends have done in my whole life. I'm so glad to have found people like you, people who quickly have become family. Thank you for the random drop-ins to check on my health, the walks and trips to the park so I can breathe fresh air, and for all the nights you invited me over for dinner. You have been an oasis in an otherwise hectic season of my life.

I want to thank my book mentor Cristina Curp for scheduling calls to keep this project on track and for checking in on my mental well-being. I couldn't have done this without you.

I want to give a massive shoutout to my girl Jamie Lou, my story editor turned gal pal. I appreciate everything you've done for me and this book.

And finally, I want to acknowledge my team at Row House Publishing. Without you, this book wouldn't exist. Special shoutout to Rebekah and Justin Borucki for making the work feel joyful. You have made this project come to life and exceed all my expectations. I am truly blessed to be a part of this team.

INDEX